The Original
Summer Bridge Activities™

Fifth to Sixth Grade

SBA was created by
Michele D. Van Leeuwen

written by
Julia Ann Hobbs
Carla Dawn Fisher

illustrations by
Magen Mitchell
Amanda Sorensen

Summer Learning Staff
Clareen Arnold, Lori Davis, Melody Feist, Aimee Hansen, Christopher Kugler,
Kristina Kugler, Molly McMahon, Paul Rawlins, Liza Richards, Linda Swain

Design
Andy Carlson, Robyn Funk

Cover Art
Karen Maizel, Andy Carlson

ISBN: 978-1-59441-731-3

Super Summer Science pages © 2002 The Wild Goose Company and Carson-Dellosa.

20 19 18 17 16 15 14 13 12 11

Dear Parents,

The summer months are a perfect time to reconnect with your young scholar on many levels after a long school year. Your personal involvement is so important to your child's immediate and long-term academic success. No matter how wonderful your child's classroom experience is, your involvement outside the classroom will make it that much better!

Summer Bridge Activities™ is the original summer workbook developed to help parents support their children academically while away from school, and we strive to improve the content, the activities, and the resources to give you the highest quality summer learning materials available. Ten years ago, we introduced **Summer Bridge Activities**™ to a small group of teachers and parents after I had successfully used it to help my own child prepare for the new school year. It was a hit then, and it continues to be a hit now! Many other summer workbooks have been introduced since, but **Summer Bridge Activities**™ continues to be the one that both teachers and parents ask for most. We take our responsibility as the leader in summer education seriously and are always looking for new ways to make summer learning more fun, more motivating, and more effective to help make your child's transition to the new school year enjoyable and successful!

We are now excited to offer you even more bonus summer learning materials online at www.**SummerBridgeActivities**.com! This site has great resources for both parents and kids to use on their own and together. An expanded summer reading program where kids can post their own book reviews, writing and reading contests with great prizes, assessment tests, travel packs, and even games are a few of the additional resources that you and your child will have access to with the included **Summer Bridge Activities**™ Online Pass Code.

Summer Learning has come a long way over the last 10 years, and we are glad that you have chosen to use **Summer Bridge Activities**™ to help your children continue to discover the world around them by using the classroom skills they worked so hard to obtain!

Have a wonderful summer!

Michele Van Leeuwen and the Summer Learning Staff!

Hey Kids!

We bet you had a great school year!
Congratulations on all your hard work! We just want to say that we're proud of the great things you did this year, and we're excited to have you spend time with us over the summer. Have fun with your **Summer Bridge Activities**™ workbook, and visit us online at www.**SummerBridgeActivities**.com for more fun, cool, and exciting stuff!

Have a great summer!

The T. O. C. (Table of Contents)

Parent Letter. ii
Pass Code for Online Bonus Materials iii
Summer Bridge Activities™ Overview. iv
Maximizing **Summer Bridge Activities**™ v
Skills List vi
Summertime = Reading Time! viii
Summer Reading List ix

Section 1

Motivational Calendar. 1
Day 1–15—Daily Activities in Math, Reading, Writing, and Language. 3
Super Summer Science Section! 33

Section 2

Motivational Calendar. 35
Day 1–20—Daily Activities in Math, Reading, Writing, and Language. 37
Super Summer Science Section! 77

Section 3

Motivational Calendar. 79
Day 1–15—Daily Activities in Math, Reading, Writing, and Language. 81
Super Summer Science Section! 111

Answer Pages 113
Building Better Bodies and Behavior. 127
Certificate of Completion

Sections of SBA

- There are three sections in SBA: the first and second review, the third previews.

- Each section begins with an SBA Motivational Calendar.

- Each day your child will complete activities in reading, writing, math, or language. The activities become progressively more challenging.

- Each page is numbered by day.

Official Pass Code

ma0703r

Log on to **www.SummerBridgeActivities.com** and join!

Here's what you will find inside

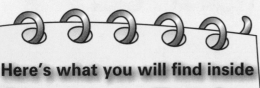

Summer Bridge Activities™

Exercises in **Summer Bridge Activities™** (SBA) are easy to understand and presented in fun and creative ways that motivate students to review familiar skills while being progressively challenged. In addition to basic skills in reading, writing, math, and language arts, **Summer Bridge Activities™** contains activities that challenge and reinforce skills in geography and science!

Daily exercises review and preview skills in reading, writing, math, language arts, social studies, with additional activities in geography and science. Exercises are divided into three sections to correlate with traditional summer vacation.

Bonus Super Summer Science pages provide hands-on science activities.

A Summer Reading List introduces some of today's popular titles as well as the classics. Kids can rate books they read and log on to www.**SummerBridgeActivities**.com to post reviews, find more great titles, and participate in national reading and writing contests!

Motivational Calendars begin each section to help motivate kids all summer long.

Discover Something New lists offer fun and creative activities that teach kids with their hands and get them active and learning.

Removable Answer Pages ensure that parents know as much as their kids!

A Certificate of Completion for parents to sign congratulates summer learners for their work and welcomes them to the grade ahead.

A grade-appropriate, official Summer Fun pass code gives kids and parents online access to more bonus games, contests, and resources at www.**SummerBridgeActivities**.com.

Here are some groups who say our books are great!

Mr. Fredrickson

Maximizing
The Original Summer Bridge Activities™

Let your middle-grade student familiarize himself with the workbook. Have him look through the pages to see what skills and exercises the book contains as well as how the book is formatted.

Agree on a time that your child will complete the daily exercises. Make sure that it is consistent and that it is a set amount of time.

Provide any necessary materials, including a pencil, ruler, dictionary, or other reference books. In addition, be prepared to use the Internet, as some activities may contain material that students need to research online.

Support your young scholar with positive guidance and direction. The activities are not meant to be tests, but rather re-enforcement. Remain positive and supportive as your child dedicates time during the summer.

Encourage your child to complete the exercises on her own or to research the material online before coming to you. However, be there if she needs you.

Encourage summertime reading! Students may get tired of reading textbooks during the school year, so use the summer months to remind them how great reading for pleasure and entertainment is!

Above all, remember to have fun with learning during the summer! You and your young scholar are being proactive with education, and you should enjoy the experience of learning outside of the classroom!

Skills List

Language Arts/Reading

- Recognizes the purpose of a written passage
- Recognizes topic sentences and main ideas
- Understands the writing process
- Understands how to write dialogue
- Demonstrates knowledge of how to brainstorm
- Can recognize and use correct punctuation
- Understands the concept of analogies
- Can recognize and use metaphor
- Understands how to use a dictionary
- Understands cause and effect
- Understands how to compare and contrast things
- Understands how words are broken up into syllables
- Can effectively use prefixes
- Can properly form possessives and plural words
- Can recognize and write complete sentences
- Recognizes subjects and predicates
- Can read and write in cursive script
- Recognizes nouns
- Recognizes verbs
- Recognizes adjectives
- Recognizes adverbs
- Recognizes subject pronouns
- Recognizes object pronouns
- Recognizes direct objects
- Can use adjectives in writing
- Can use adverbs correctly
- Recognizes compound words
- Understands how to use contractions correctly
- Can recognize and correct misspelled words
- Can write a friendly letter

Parent:

Exercises for these skills can be found inside **Summer Bridge Activities™** and can be used for extra practice. The skills lists are a great way to discover your child's strengths or what skills may need additional reinforcement.

Skills List

Math

- [ ] Uses problem-solving strategies to complete math problems
- [ ] Understands number definitions and terms
- [ ] Can use estimation to solve math problems involving weight and cost
- [ ] Understands place value
- [ ] Can sequence events
- [ ] Can measure using inches
- [ ] Can measure using centimeters
- [ ] Can identify and write fractions
- [ ] Performs three-digit addition, no regrouping
- [ ] Performs three-digit subtraction, no regrouping
- [ ] Performs two-digit addition, with regrouping
- [ ] Performs two-digit subtraction, with regrouping
- [ ] Performs three-digit addition, with regrouping
- [ ] Performs three-digit subtraction, with regrouping
- [ ] Performs four-digit addition
- [ ] Performs five-digit addition
- [ ] Can solve story problems involving addition, subtraction, and multiplication
- [ ] Performs two-digit multiplication
- [ ] Performs two-digit division
- [ ] Performs three-digit multiplication
- [ ] Performs three-digit division
- [ ] Can find common multiples for numbers
- [ ] Can add, subtract, multiply, and divide with decimals
- [ ] Can read and use tables and graphs (pie, line, bar)
- [ ] Understands basic geometry facts and terms
- [ ] Can find perimeter and area
- [ ] Can do simple geometry and calculate angles
- [ ] Can use deductive reasoning to find missing numbers
- [ ] Understands percentages
- [ ] Can write decimals as percentages and percentages as decimals
- [ ] Recognizes negative and positive numbers

Summertime = Reading Time!

Your young scholars are now at a place where reading should be an activity that they do on a regular basis. It is important that they know how to explore books, titles, and authors and understand where they can go to find books and other reading materials. As adults we often assume that our children know where to go because of their involvement in school activities and programs; however, we need to support and encourage their love of reading at home as well.

Books to Read

The Summer Reading List has a variety of titles, including some found in the Accelerated Reader Program.

We recommend parents read to pre-kindergarten through 1st grade children 5–10 minutes each day and then ask questions about the story to reinforce comprehension. For higher grade levels, we suggest the following daily reading times: grades 1–2, 10–20 min.; grades 2–3, 20–30 min.; grades 3–4, 30–45 min.; grades 4–8, 45–60 min.

It is important to decide an amount of reading time and write it on the SBA Motivational Calendar.

Here are a few ideas on encouraging reading in your middle-grade students this summer and fostering more enthusiasm for the adventure of reading outside the classroom.

Lead by example! Show your kids how much you enjoy reading by doing it yourself. Curl up with a book where your kids can see you reading—and enjoying it!

Ask your children thought-provoking questions about topics that interest them, and encourage them to explore them through books. Have them research titles online and go to the bookstore or library to check out the books they find.

Talk to your children about books that you were interested in when you were their age. You may even find that they have heard of some of the same books!

Form a reading group and take turns choosing books to read. Give yourselves a couple of weeks or even a month to read, and then plan a lunch or dinner where you can discuss the book with each other.

Look for programs offered by your local library. These don't need to have anything to do with reading but can be talks about local artists, film, and even authors themselves. Get your kids interested in topics that they will want to learn more about, and encourage them to find out more on their own through books and literature.

Summer Bridge Activities™

Summer Reading List

Fill in the stars and rate your favorite (and not so favorite) books here and online at
www.SummerBridgeActivities.com!

1 = I struggled to finish this book.
2 = I thought this book was pretty good.
3 = I thought this book rocked!
4 = I want to read this book again and again!

The Wish Giver: Three Tales of Coven Tree

Brittain, Bill

Walk Two Moons

Creech, Sharon

The Midwife's Apprentice

Cushman, Karen

Jacob's Rescue: A Holocaust Story

Drucker, Malka

The Spoon in the Bathroom Wall

Johnston, Tony

A magical take on the Arthurian legend. Martha Snapdragon and her father live in the boiler room of Horace E. Bloggins school. When a mysterious golden spoon appears in the wall of the boys' bathroom, things quickly begin to change...

Regarding the Sink

Klise, Kate

Artist Florence Waters is supposed to design a new cafeteria sink for Geyser Creek Middle School. Unfortunately, Ms. Waters is missing.

Ella Enchanted

Levine, Gail Carson

Chronicles of Narnia Series

Lewis, C.S.

Little House on Rocky Ridge

MacBride, Roger Lea

The Moorchild

McGraw, Eloise

Across America on an Emigrant Train
Murphy, Jim ☆☆☆☆☆

The War with Grandpa
Smith, Robert Kimmel ☆☆☆☆☆

Voices after Midnight
Peck, Richard E. ☆☆☆☆☆

Miracles on Maple Hill
Sorensen, Virginia ☆☆☆☆☆

Me, My Goat, and My Sister's Wedding
Pevsner, Stella ☆☆☆☆☆

Call It Courage
Sperry, Armstrong ☆☆☆☆☆

The View from the Cherry Tree
Roberts, Willo Davis ☆☆☆☆☆

The Dog on Barkham Street
Stolz, Mary ☆☆☆☆☆

The Fifth of March
Rinaldi, Ann ☆☆☆☆☆

Journey to Topaz
Uchida, Yoshiko ☆☆☆☆☆

Missing May
Rylant, Cynthia ☆☆☆☆☆

This touching Newbery Medal winner follows Summer and Uncle Ob as they struggle to deal with their grief after Aunt May, Ob's wife, dies.

A Visit to William Blake's Inn: Poems for Innocent and Experienced Travelers
Willard, Nancy ☆☆☆☆☆

The Rainbow People
Yep, Laurence ☆☆☆☆☆

Join the SBA Kids Summer Reading Club!

Quick! Get Mom or Dad to help you log on and join the SBA Kids Summer Reading Club. You can find more great books, tell your friends about your favorite titles, and even win cool prizes! Log on to www.SummerBridgeActivities.com and sign up today.

Cover illustration © 1992 by Reba Ade from MISSING MAY by Cynthia Rylant. Published by Orchard Books/Scholastic Inc. Reprinted by permission.

Summer Bridge Activities™

Motivational Calendar

Month

My parents and I decided that if I complete
15 days of **Summer Bridge Activities**™ and
read _____ minutes a day, my incentive/reward will be:

_____

Child's Signature _____ Parent's Signature_____

Day 1	☆	📖	____	**Day 9**	☆	📖	____
Day 2	☆	📖	____	**Day 10**	☆	📖	____
Day 3	☆	📖	____	**Day 11**	☆	📖	____
Day 4	☆	📖	____	**Day 12**	☆	📖	____
Day 5	☆	📖	____	**Day 13**	☆	📖	____
Day 6	☆	📖	____	**Day 14**	☆	📖	____
Day 7	☆	📖	____	**Day 15**	☆	📖	____
Day 8	☆	📖	____				

Child: Color the ☆ for daily activities completed.
Color the 📖 for daily reading completed.

Parent: Initial the ____ when all activities are complete.

1   © Summer Bridge Activities™ 5–6

Discover Something New!

1. Describe what you look like and write it down.

2. Polish a pair of your mom's or dad's shoes and put a love note in the toe.

3. Visit a sick neighbor, friend, or relative.

4. In the evening, look at the sky. Find the first star and make a wish.

5. Pick one of your favorite foods and learn how to make it.

Fun Activity Ideas to Go Along with the First Section!

6. Make a picnic lunch for two; then invite a friend over and have a picnic in your backyard.

7. Start a diary.

8. Ask your mom or dad for an old map and plan a trip. Decide on a destination and highlight your route. Figure out how many days it would take, where you would stop, and what you would like to see. Use the legend on the map to help you make these decisions.

9. Hold a fire drill in your home.

10. Find some old socks, buttons, yarn, and a needle and thread. Make puppets and name them. Then find a cardboard box and paint it. Cut a hole in the front to put the puppets through and put on a puppet show for younger children.

11. Feed the birds.

12. Learn how to do something you have always wanted to do, like play the guitar, cross-stitch, rollerblade, cook pizza, train your dog, etc.

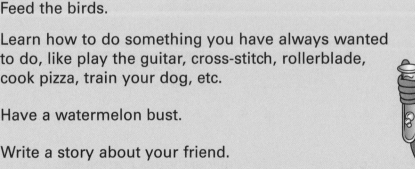

13. Have a watermelon bust.

14. Write a story about your friend.

15. Make a pitcher of lemonade or tropical Kool-Aid and sell it in front of your house.

Use the following information to solve problems dealing with place value.

billions			millions			thousands					
hundred-billions	ten-billions	billions	hundred-millions	ten-millions	millions	hundred-thousands	ten-thousands	thousands	hundreds	tens	ones

Remember: In numeral form, commas separate millions, thousands, etc.

Write the following in expanded form. The first one is done for you.

1. 72,584,361

   70,000,000 + 2,000,000 + 500,000 + 80,000 + 4,000 + 300 + 60 + 1

2. 37,126,489

3. 56,487,320,960

4. 90,675,409,783

Write the following using the correct word form. The first one is done for you.

5. 826,531,947,683

   Eight hundred twenty-six billion five hundred thirty-one million nine hundred forty-seven thousand six hundred eighty-three

6. 406,723,891,534

7. 861,750,432,971

8. 900,076,580,035

A metaphor compares two different things. Here are a few metaphors:

Homework is a sweaty sock: it stinks!

People are mirrors; you can see yourself in them.

Sleep is a stone, quiet and still.

Write your own metaphor by comparing two different things.

1. Sleep is _____

2. Life is _____

3. Anger is _____

4. Happiness is _____

5. Friendship is _____

Communication skills are very important. Read the sentences below. Rate yourself between 1 (lowest) and 5 (highest) on how well you communicate. Then answer the following questions.

Your rating: _____

1. I speak clearly and loudly so others can hear what I am saying.   yes   no

2. I express my feelings.   yes   no

3. I try to think before I speak so I will not hurt others' feelings.   yes   no

4. I listen when others are talking.   yes   no

5. I do not share secrets that others have trusted me to keep.   yes   no

• What areas of communication are your strong points?   _____

• What areas of communication do you need to improve?   _____

What's in a Number? Write a definition and some examples of the following number words or terms.

Whole numbers	Number integers	Prime numbers	Composite numbers
_____	_____	_____	_____
_____	_____	_____	_____
_____	_____	_____	_____
_____	_____	_____	_____
_____	_____	_____	_____
_____	_____	_____	_____

Label as many states on this map as you can.

Read the following paragraphs and answer the questions.

Timbuktu is a small trading town in central Mali. It was established around A.D. 1100 and is located near the southern edge of the Sahara Desert. It was a trading post for products from North and West Africa. Camel caravans from the north traded salt, cloth, cowrie shells, and copper. The dealers in Timbuktu exchanged the goods for gold, kola nuts, ivory, and slaves that they got from the south.

Timbuktu's location left it open to attack, and control of the city changed many times. It has been ruled by the Mali Empire, the Songhai Empire, Morocco, nomads, and others. France controlled it from 1893 until 1960. However, it has declined in importance and population since the early 1600s. Many of its mud and brick buildings are eroding and are half-buried in the sand.

1. What is the topic of the first paragraph?

2. What is the main idea of the first paragraph?

3. What is the topic of the second paragraph?

4. What is the main idea of the second paragraph?

Match the kind of writing with the purpose of the writing.

_____ newspaper article about the war in Iraq

A. explains how to do something

B. entertains you

_____ book about how to collect stamps

C. gives an opinion about something

_____ comic book

D. gives you directions

_____ phone book

E. gets you to buy something

_____ Internet pop-up advertisement

F. gives you information

_____ *The Lord of the Rings*

G. tells a story

_____ a biography about a movie star

Estimation and Addition. Estimate each sum by using your knowledge of rounding off numbers.

1. 45 + 32 _____

2. 74 + 23 _____

3. 91 + 57 _____

4. 37 + 83 _____

5. 389 + 412 _____

6. 278 + 582 _____

7. 222 + 387 _____

8. 625 + 371 _____

9. 432 + 929 _____

10. 351 + 476 _____

11. 948 + 511 _____

12. 999 + 808 _____

13. 2,735 + 4,960 _____

14. 5,429 + 2,099 _____

15. 10,364 + 3,910 _____

16. 22,100 + 30,439 _____

17. 34,433 + 16,377 _____

18. 110,345 + 7,630 _____

19. 205,933 + 460,362 _____

20. 711,393 + 202,501 _____

Match the correct capital with each state.

_____ Alabama	_____ Nebraska	**a.** Montpelier	**n.** Salem
_____ Arizona	_____ New Hampshire	**b.** Honolulu	**o.** Boston
_____ California	_____ New Mexico	**c.** Hartford	**p.** Pierre
_____ Connecticut	_____ North Carolina	**d.** Lincoln	**q.** Sacramento
_____ Florida	_____ Ohio	**e.** Columbus	**r.** Frankfort
_____ Hawaii	_____ Oregon	**f.** Madison	**s.** Montgomery
_____ Illinois	_____ Rhode Island	**g.** St. Paul	**t.** Augusta
_____ Iowa	_____ South Dakota	**h.** Springfield	**u.** Raleigh
_____ Kentucky	_____ Texas	**i.** Phoenix	**v.** Austin
_____ Maine	_____ Vermont	**j.** Des Moines	**w.** Concord
_____ Massachusetts	_____ Washington	**k.** Providence	**x.** Tallahassee
_____ Minnesota	_____ Wisconsin	**l.** Olympia	**y.** Jefferson City
_____ Missouri		**m.** Santa Fe	

Look up the word <u>dramatize</u> in a dictionary and answer the following questions.

1. What are the guide words on the page?

2. How many meanings are listed for the word?

3. Write the word. Show the special spelling.

4. How many syllables does the word have?

5. What does dramatize mean in this sentence?
   Do you always have to <u>dramatize</u> everything, Annie?

6. Write the other forms of the word given in the dictionary and tell what part of speech they are.

7. List two other words on the same page as <u>dramatize</u>. Show the special spelling.

"I" Messages. A way to share feelings is to use an "I" message. An "I" message includes an action, effect, and feeling. For example, a friend is coming to your house so you can go to a show. He or she is late. You might say to your friend, "Because you were late [action], I thought we would miss the show [effect]. I was angry [feeling]."

Read the scenarios below and write an "I" message.

1. You find out that a friend is telling lies about you.
   [action]
   [effect]
   [feeling]

2. Your parents have given you a special present.
   [action]
   [effect]
   [feeling]

3. You thought your friend was to meet you at 2:00, but he didn't come until 3:00.
   [action]
   [effect]
   [feeling]

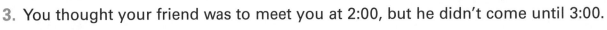

Field Trip.

The students at Franklin Elementary School are going on a field trip to the Museum of Natural History. Three thousand sixty-eight students are going on Wednesday, and 2,864 are going on Thursday. Mr. Rand, the principal, wants to order special school name tags that come in packs of 1,000. Each package costs $5.25.

How many packages does Mr. Rand need to order? _____

What steps did you use to solve the problem?

Could you have used any of these ways or a combination of ways to find the answer?

a. mental math   d. subtraction

b. estimation   e. place value

c. addition   f. guessed

What information was essential to know before you solved the problem?

What information was not necessary to know?

* *

Match the correct capital with each state.

_____ Alaska	_____ Nevada	a. Salt Lake City	n. Helena
_____ Arkansas	_____ New Jersey	b. Lansing	o. Cheyenne
_____ Colorado	_____ New York	c. Bismarck	p. Topeka
_____ Delaware	_____ North Dakota	d. Annapolis	q. Richmond
_____ Georgia	_____ Oklahoma	e. Nashville	r. Trenton
_____ Idaho	_____ Pennsylvania	f. Juneau	s. Boise
_____ Indiana	_____ South Carolina	g. Harrisburg	t. Albany
_____ Kansas	_____ Tennessee	h. Dover	u. Jackson
_____ Louisiana	_____ Utah	i. Carson City	v. Columbia
_____ Maryland	_____ Virginia	j. Little Rock	w. Baton Rouge
_____ Michigan	_____ West Virginia	k. Indianapolis	x. Atlanta
_____ Mississippi	_____ Wyoming	l. Denver	y. Charleston
_____ Montana		m. Oklahoma City	

Write a sentence for each compound word below.

- levelheaded
- hand-me-downs
- halfhearted
- lifesaver
- sightseers
- well-balanced
- self-addressed
- wholesale

1. _____

2. _____

3. _____

4. _____

5. _____

6. _____

7. _____

8. _____

Study the chart of the skeletal system below. Go outside with a partner. Lie flat on the sidewalk and have your partner outline your body. Draw the skeletal system in the outline of your body. Label as many bones as you can.

femur
humerus
scapula
radius
ulna
metatarsals
fibula
tibia
rib
vertebrae
ilium
skull
patella
sternum

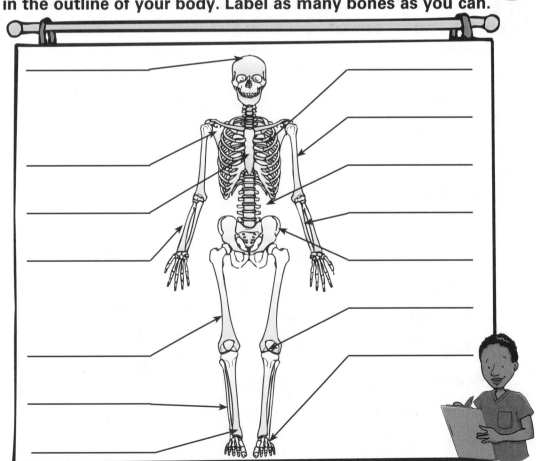

Estimation with Sums and Differences.
Estimate the sum or difference first; then find the actual sum or difference.

1. 8,666 +9,346 estimate _____ actual _____	**2.** 7,543 +2,396 estimate _____ actual _____	**3.** 3,693 +1,690 estimate _____ actual _____	**4.** 54,561 +36,287 estimate _____ actual _____
5. 34,865 +62,444 estimate _____ actual _____	**6.** 47,267 +55,085 estimate _____ actual _____	**7.** 65,639 +53,263 estimate _____ actual _____	**8.** 28,790 +83,964 estimate _____ actual _____
9. 5,394 −2,587 estimate _____ actual _____	**10.** 3,368 −2,139 estimate _____ actual _____	**11.** 69,293 −22,887 estimate _____ actual _____	**12.** 125,394 −69,831 estimate _____ actual _____

Below are the stressed syllables of some spelling words. Write the other syllables, and then write the words in cursive. Each blank stands for a letter. The first one is done for you.

purchaser	chosen	diamond	appearance
refund	measure	attention	manager
magazine	~~January~~	trillion	causing

1. Jan´*uary*   *January* _____

2. __ __ pear´ __ __ __ __ __   _____

3. __ __ ten´ __ __ __ __ __   _____

4. cho´ __ __ __   _____

5. pur´ __ __ __ __ __ __ __   _____

6. di´ __ __ __ __ __ __   _____

7. re´ __ __ __ __   _____

8. mag´ __ __ __ __ __ __   _____

9. tril´ __ __ __ __   _____

10. man´ __ __ __ __ __   _____

11. mea´ __ __ __ __ __   _____

12. caus´ __ __ __   _____

Some sentences have a clue word to help show the cause-effect relationship. Fill in the blanks with clue words. Then write the cause and effect.

Our school was closed today <u>because</u> of the bad snowstorm we had last night.

Cause: *Bad snowstorm.*

Effect: *School was closed.*

1. It snowed all day, _____ the ground was white.

   Cause:_____

   Effect: _____

2. Our electricity went off last night, _____ we went out to dinner.

   Cause:_____

   Effect: _____

3. _____ Joe left the gate unlatched, all the cattle were out in the road.

   Cause:_____

   Effect: _____

4. Scott woke up with the flu today; _____ , he had to miss school.

   Cause:_____

   Effect: _____

Science—Structure of the Earth.
Label the different layers of the earth with the terms below.
Use the same terms to complete the sentences below.

1. The core of the earth has two parts.

   The _____ is liquid.

   The _____ is solid.

center of the earth	**crust**
inner core	**mantle**
outer core	**lithosphere**

2. One reason the crust and _____ are brittle is because they are the outermost and coldest layers of the earth.

3. The top layer of the earth is the _____.

4. The _____ is extremely hot and is the thickest layer.

5. As the _____ is approached, pressure and temperature increase.

Mental Math for Multiples of 10, 100, and 1,000.
Remember to use mental math!

1. 7 × 10 = _____
2. 16 × 10 = _____
3. 10 × 92 = _____

4. 100 × 8 = _____
5. 50 × 50 = _____
6. 7 × 600 = _____

7. 500 × 200 = _____
8. 5 × 900 = _____
9. 70 × 60 = _____

10. 30 × 400 = _____
11. 200 × 300 = _____
12. 400 × 600 = _____

13. 8 × 1,000 = _____
14. 9 × 3,000 = _____
15. 30 × 5,000 = _____

16. 9,000 × 700 = _____
17. 7,000 × 50 = _____
18. 60 × 8,000 = _____

19. 52 × 2,000 = _____
20. 400 × 300 = _____
21. 5,000 × 50 = _____

22. 250 × 200 = _____
23. 15,000 × 30 = _____
24. 200,000 × 40 = _____

Healthy Lifestyles.
Fill in the chart of acts and consequences. Using the last two lines, fill in two acts that you may do and what consequences follow.

Acts	Consequences
1. Do not eat breakfast	
2. Cheat on test	
3.	Feel good about yourself
4.	Have a lot of energy
5. Take a shower every day	
6. Adult catches your friend smoking	
7. Visit the elderly	
8. Say NO to drugs	
9.	
10.	

Show the syllables by leaving a space between them. Then write <u>long</u>, <u>short</u>, <u>schwa</u>, or <u>silent</u> for the vowel sound in each syllable. Remember, the schwa sound is usually heard in the unstressed syllable. Use a dictionary if you need help.

EXAMPLE: terrific *ter ri fic schwa short short* _____

1. jackal _____

2. liable _____

3. volcano _____

4. that _____

5. attraction _____

6. billow _____

7. paralysis _____

8. identify _____

9. mold _____

10. victory _____

The Muscular System and Nervous System.
Fill in the blanks with the correct word.

cerebrum	involuntary muscles	nervous system	
voluntary muscles	cerebellum	contracts	spinal cord

1. Muscles you can control are called _____.

2. When one muscle in a pair _____, or shortens, the other muscle relaxes.

3. _____ are muscles that work automatically, such as the heart.

4. The _____ is the network of cells that receive and send messages to and from the brain and spinal cord to every part of your body.

5. The part of your brain that controls your learning and memory is the_____.

6. The _____ controls how your muscles work together.

7. The _____ extends from the base of the brain down your back and is involved with all senses.

Multiplying by 2- and 3-Digit Numbers.

Remember:

```
   218            429            293
 ×  36          × 375          × 704
 1308           2145           1172
 654            3003           000
 7848           1287           2051
               160875         206272
```

1.	826 × 47	2.	584 × 29	3.	249 × 63	4.	973 × 51
5.	670 × 94	6.	776 × 68	7.	845 × 77	8.	392 × 82
9.	628 × 274	10.	831 × 347	11.	609 × 149	12.	586 × 781

Possessive and plural forms of many nouns sound alike but are different. An 's can make the base word noun become a singular possessive. For example: All the <u>players</u> (plural) had coats that looked the same, but one <u>player's</u> (singular possessive) coat was ripped in the back. In the following sentences, cross out the plurals and possessives that are incorrect. Write them correctly at the right of the sentences. If they are right, just write "correct."

1. All the news <u>reporter's</u> decided to stay at the Brookgreen Inn. _____

2. Ten <u>driver's</u> went out on the job this morning, but only nine returned. _____

3. One <u>drivers</u> truck was stuck in a huge snowdrift. _____

4. The <u>announcer's</u> voice sounded awful this morning. _____

5. Many <u>authors</u> had a convention last year to come up with new ideas for books. _____

6. The <u>organizer's</u> of this party can be proud of themselves. _____

Sequence. Read this paragraph; then write the main points in the correct order. The third one is done for you.

Traveling Spiders

The baby wolf spider rides on its mother's back. Jumping spiders travel by ballooning. They raise their abdomens so the wind can pull silk threads from their spinnerets. The wind then lifts the little spiders into the air like balloons on strings. Fisher spiders are very light-weight, so they can travel by walking on water. Crab spiders walk backwards and sidewards. All spiders can make and travel on a dragline (a silk thread).

1. _____

2. _____

3. *Fisher spiders can walk on water.* _____

4. _____

5. _____

Digestive System. Put the steps of the digestive process in the proper sequence.

_____ Food moves to the small intestine.

_____ The tongue pushes food down the esophagus.

_____ Undigested food passes out of the body through the anus.

_____ Villi in the small intestine absorb digested food into the bloodstream.

_____ Teeth and saliva start to change food.

_____ Undigested food moves to the large intestine, or colon.

_____ Food goes to the stomach where it is further broken down.

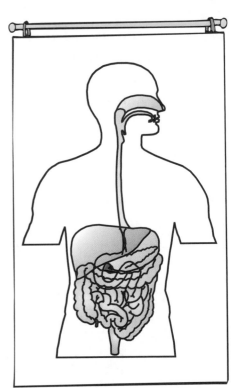

Add, Subtract, or Multiply. Find the answer to each of the following story problems and tell which operation you used to solve the problem.

1. You can make 36 single-dipped ice cream cones out of one gallon of ice cream. If you have 12 different flavors of one-gallon ice cream containers, how many cones do you need to use all of the ice cream? _____

2. Mrs. Stone hand-dipped 425 chocolates the first of May, 592 the middle of May, and 143 the last part of May. How many chocolates did she make in May? _____

3. Farmer Tim sold 4,987 pounds of potatoes last year and 12,709 pounds this year. Next year he hopes to do even better. How many more pounds of potatoes did he sell this year than last year? _____

4. Denim shorts sell for $27.59 a pair at Lornet Department Store. Its regular denim jeans sell for $12.18 more than its denim shorts. How much do the store's regular denim jeans cost? _____

5. If each person in the United States drank 42 gallons of milk a year, and each gallon cost $1.98, how much would each person spend on milk a year? _____

6. Gloria bought 25 pairs of socks at $5.80 a pair. If her mother gave her $500, would she have enough money left to buy 6 pairs of shoes at $30.00 each? _____

Look in an atlas. Which states contain the following latitude and longitude?

1. 40° N, 110° W _____

2. 35° N, 110° W _____

3. 35° N, 120° W _____

4. 40° N, 83° W _____

5. 33° N, 87° W _____

6. What is the latitude and longitude of one corner of your state? _____

7. What is the latitude and longitude of your city or town? _____

Context clues help you learn new words and their meanings. Use the context clues in the following sentences to tell what the underlined words mean.

1. Mary <u>feigned</u> surprise when her friends had a birthday party for her.

   feigned— _____

2. My <u>colleagues</u> and I work together on many new projects.

   colleagues— _____

3. Maurice looks at his watch often to make sure he is always <u>punctual</u>.

   punctual— _____

4. Joseph, a <u>philatelist</u>, has a large collection of stamps.

   philatelist— _____

5. The pig napping in the mud was hardly able to <u>bestir</u> itself for its dinner.

   bestir— _____

Read the following passage and answer the questions below.

Englishman Sir Walter Raleigh wanted to start a colony in the New World (North America). In 1585, Raleigh sent colonists to what is now North Carolina. The colonists did not want to work and almost starved to death. They were taken back to England. Two years later a second group of colonists sailed over to the same place as the previous colonists. They worked very hard to survive.

Because of a war involving England, Raleigh lost track of the colonists. In 1591, a ship from England finally arrived to check on the colonists, but the colonists had disappeared! There was no sign of life. All the sailors found were some empty trunks, rotted maps, and the word CROATOAN carved on the doorpost of the fort. Croatoan was an island 100 miles south of the Lost Colony. No one knows if the colonists were attacked by the Croatoan Indians or if the settlers went to live on Croatoan Island. The Lost Colony has been a great mystery in American history.

1. How many years has it been since the first colony settled in North Carolina?

2. How many years did it take to send a ship to check on the second set of colonists?

3. Why was this colony called the Lost Colony?

4. State what you think might have happened to the Lost Colony.

5. Think of a title that would be appropriate for this passage.

Find the quotient by dividing whole numbers.

EXAMPLE:

$$\begin{array}{r} 92 \text{ R } 1 \\ 9\overline{)829} \\ \underline{81} \\ 19 \\ \underline{18} \\ 1 \end{array}$$

$829 \div 9 = 92$ with a remainder of 1

Use mental math or scratch paper if needed.

1. $8\overline{)231}$　　2. $5\overline{)3,305}$　　3. $83\overline{)4,978}$　　4. $57\overline{)92,831}$

5. $4\overline{)394}$　　6. $75\overline{)675}$　　7. $59\overline{)4,538}$　　8. $40\overline{)73,847}$

9. $9\overline{)894}$　　10. $70\overline{)5,844}$　　11. $41\overline{)3,613}$　　12. $62\overline{)79,365}$

Spelling. Find the word that is misspelled in each row and spell it correctly. Use a dictionary if you need help.

1.	refund	remodel	decode	previw	_____
2.	deposet	pretend	deflate	pace	_____
3.	mold	respond	brutel	revise	_____
4.	fiction	grieff	unsafe	equip	_____
5.	transfer	defend	truthful	penlty	_____
6.	prdict	decide	gossip	fragile	_____
7.	beware	precice	porches	capital	_____
8.	leashes	cipher	volt	climack	_____
9.	month	friendly	wrench	businiss	_____
10.	jiant	angle	guest	greet	_____

Remember: Prefixes are added to the beginning of base words.
Add prefixes to these base words. Use as many prefixes as you can
with the base words and see how many words you can make.
Use prefixes <u>mis-</u>, <u>re-</u>, <u>un-</u>, <u>non-</u>, and <u>pre-</u>.

EXAMPLE:

view *preview review* _____   trace _____

name _____   heat   _____

spell _____   cut   _____

treat _____   turn   _____

stop   _____   read   _____

sure   _____   fit   _____

call   _____   place _____

Choose one word for each of the prefixes and write a sentence for it.

mis   1. _____

re   2. _____

un   3. _____

non   4. _____

pre   5. _____

**Circulatory System. Label the different parts of the heart with the terms
listed. Color the side of the heart that has oxygen-rich blood red.
Color the side of the heart where the blood is lacking oxygen blue.**

- aorta
- left ventricle
- tricuspid valve
- cardiac septum
- left atrium
- aortic valve
- pulmonary valve
- right ventricle
- right atrium
- bicuspid valve
- pulmonary artery
- pulmonary vein

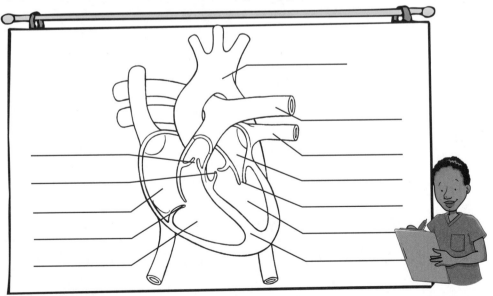

Mixed Practice. Be sure to watch the signs.
You can use mental math or scratch paper if needed.

1. 793 × 27 = _____

2. 7,133 ÷ 8 = _____

3. 4,036 × 9 = _____

4. 143 + 973 = _____

5. 72,483 + 56,774 = _____

6. 8)‾9,696‾ = _____

7. 63,459 − 21,365 = _____

8. 90)‾48,713‾ = _____

9. 569,040 ÷ 8 = _____

10. 53,907 × 6 = _____

11. 483 × 175 = _____

12. 763,947 − 244,398 = _____

13. 45)‾29,705‾ = _____

14. 14,008 ÷ 60 = _____

15. $678.14 + $990.27 = _____

16. 3,046 × 70 = _____

17. 34,148 + 95,228 = _____

18. 573 + 4,935 + 7,340 = _____

19. 75)‾566,212‾ = _____

20. 3,804 × 43 = _____

Matter exists in three states: solid, liquid, and gas.
Put the following words in the appropriate categories.

butter	lava	oxygen	water
box	dust	ice	radon
milk	juice	nitrogen	vapor

Solid	Liquid	Gas

Water can be in three different states: solid-ice, liquid-water, gas-vapor.
See if you can come up with some items in your home that can be in more than one state.

Solid	Liquid	Gas

You have taken two kinds of tests in the past year: <u>essay</u> and <u>objective</u> tests. When you take an <u>essay</u> test you write out the answers. When you take an <u>objective</u> test you have multiple-choice, true-false, matching, and completion questions. When you take a test, read the directions carefully before you begin. Think about how much time you should take for each question and then begin. Answer the following questions and tell what kind of test they would be on. Also, if the question is from an objective test, write the type of question.

1. Match the words below to their meaning.

equip	confused noise
clatter	furnish
penalty	to ask for advice
consult	punishment

Kind of test _____ Kind of question _____

2. Write a paragraph about the produce grown in the state where you live.

_____

_____

_____

Kind of test _____ Kind of question _____

3. Fill in the blanks.

a. Most cars run on a fuel called _____.

b. _____ is candy made with milk, sugar, chocolate, and butter.

c. _____ _____ is famous for his animated movies.

d. This state does not border any other state or nation. It is _____.

Kind of test _____ Kind of question _____

4. Write <u>F</u> for false, <u>T</u> for true.

a. All mammals live on land. _____

b. After the Industrial Revolution, many people moved to the cities. _____

c. Eli Whitney invented the cotton gin. _____

d. A census worker helps find out how many people live in the United States. _____

Kind of test _____ Kind of question _____

Multiples and Common Multiples.

Remember: A <u>multiple</u> is a number exactly divisible by another number.   6 12 18 24 30 are multiples of 6.

List 5 or 6 multiples for the following numbers.

1. 5 _____

2. 10 _____

3. 9 _____

4. 12 _____

5. 3 _____

6. 2 _____

Remember: The common multiples for 2 and 4 are 4, 8, 12, or other "numbers in common."

List 3 common multiples for these numbers.

7. 3 and 4 _____

8. 4 and 7 _____

9. 5 and 10 _____

10. 6 and 8 _____

11. 2 and 9 _____

12. 5 and 6 _____

13. What is the least common multiple for 2 and 9? _____

14. For 5 and 6? _____   15. For 3 and 4? _____   16. For 8 and 10? _____

Refusal skills help a person say NO to risky behaviors and situations. Here are some refusal skills you can use:

- Say No firmly and clearly.
- Walk away if a person continues to pressure you.
- Suggest an alternative activity.
- Tell an adult you trust if you are continually pressured.
- Explain the consequences.

Read the following situations below. How would you respond to each situation? Use some of the refusal skills listed above.

1. Your friend's older sister has a pack of cigarettes in her bedroom. Your friend dares you to try one.

2. While at the store, you see a video that your really want to watch. A friend suggests you hide the video in your coat and take it home.

3. Your friend didn't study for the test today. He wants you to let him look at your paper during the test.

Writing Complete Sentences. <u>Remember</u>: A complete sentence expresses a complete thought. If it does not express a complete thought it is called a sentence fragment. A complete sentence needs to tell whom or what the sentence is about and what happened to the whom or what.

Match the sentence fragments to make complete sentences.

1. Folklore is passed   on your head?

2. The early cattle ranchers   escaped from its cage.

3. Jodie rides her   drove their cattle to the market.

4. The snake in the science corner   from generation to generation.

5. Can you balance a book   bike to school most days.

For each of the following, write <u>F</u> if it is a sentence fragment or <u>S</u> if it is a complete sentence.

1. All of my friends like spaghetti. _____   2. Answered the most questions. _____

3. Went camping last summer. _____   4. Mr. Able turned on the lights. _____

5. Collects signatures for the P.T.A. _____   6. Is Dr. Gold going to put? _____

Colonies in the New World.

Many colonists came over by boat to settle in the New World. Make a list of the supplies these adventuresome colonists would need. Write them on the scroll. Try to write as many items as you can!

Analyze the list you made. Circle in red the most important supplies one would need. Underline in blue the supplies that are of medium importance. Cross out in green the supplies that would not be necessary.

Remember: The first step when adding or subtracting decimals is to line up the decimals. If the number of decimal places is not the same, you can attach zeros to the end of a number to make it easier.

EXAMPLE:

$$3.45 + 5.923 = \begin{array}{r} 3.450 \\ + 5.923 \\ \hline 9.373 \end{array}$$

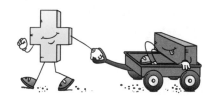

Solve the problems.

1. 18.91 + 11.5 = _____
2. 3.806 + 5.29 = _____
3. 437.7 + 13.906 = _____
4. 42.881 + 8.96 = _____
5. 34.09 – 9.407 = _____
6. 185.04 – 165.9 = _____
7. 379.76 – 37.435 = _____
8. $224.00 – $116.98 = _____
9. 49.071 + 23.015 = _____
10. 85.089 – 34.12 = _____

Analogies show relationships between words, such as <u>preview</u> is to <u>previewed</u> as <u>decide</u> is to <u>decided</u>, or <u>hear</u> is to <u>ear</u> as <u>talk</u> is to <u>mouth</u>.

Write an analogy for each of the following comparisons.

1. <u>Blue</u> is to <u>color</u> as <u>nutmeg</u> is to _____.
2. <u>Griddle</u> is to <u>pancake</u> as <u>pot</u> is to _____.
3. <u>Author</u> is to <u>book</u> as <u>artist</u> is to _____.
4. <u>Business</u> is to <u>businesses</u> as <u>address</u> is to _____.
5. <u>Research</u> is to <u>researcher</u> as <u>garden</u> is to _____.
6. <u>Breakfast</u> is to <u>lunch</u> as <u>morning</u> is to _____.
7. <u>Control</u> is to <u>controllable</u> as <u>reason</u> is to _____.
8. <u>TV</u> is to <u>commercial</u> as <u>magazine</u> is to _____.
9. <u>Sad</u> is to <u>cry</u> as <u>shout</u> is to _____.
10. <u>Manager</u> is to <u>store</u> as <u>principal</u> is to _____.

is to

as

is to

A <u>subject</u> tells what or whom the sentence is about.
A <u>predicate</u> tells about the subject.

Listed below are some complete predicates.
Write a complete subject to go with them.

1. _____ fascinated Megan.

2. _____ need water.

3. _____ collapsed suddenly.

4. _____ misplaced his new watch.

5. _____ know how to operate the computers.

Listed below are some complete subjects.
Write a complete predicate to go with them.

6. The package _____.

7. A team of horses_____.

8. The famous actor _____.

9. Sarah and Julie _____.

10. Anthills_____.

An <u>entry word</u> is a word you look up in the dictionary. It is the simplest
form of the word. If you want to find out what *costly* means, you
would look up the word *cost* in the dictionary.

What would the entry word be for each of these words?

1. celebrated *celebrate*_____

2. happier_____

3. chilly _____

4. classical _____

5. faster_____

6. couples_____

7. deformed_____

Multiplying Whole Numbers and Decimals. Remember to put the decimal point in the correct place in the product.

1. 0.12
    × 6

2. 0.08
    × 7

3. 4.6
    × 3

4. 5.05
    × 8

5. 6.5
    × 13

6. 1.906
    × 28

7. 7.0216
    × 52

8. 6.65
    × 77

9. 5.364
    × 93

10. 359.073
    × 24

11. 5.9081
    × 71

12. 12.504
    × 99

13. 8.709
    × 56

14. 27.035
    × 93

15. Jan works delivering pizza and gets paid $37.40 a night. She works 23 nights each month. How much does Jan earn each month? _____

16. Jake works at a grocery store. He gets paid $8.65 an hour for each hour he works. He usually works 37 hours a week. How much does he earn in a week? _____ How much would he earn in 4 weeks? _____

Find the next number in the number patterns below.

1. 4, 8, 16, 32, 64, ____

2. 1, 4, 7, 6, 9, 12, 11, ____

3. 1, 4, 7, 10, 13, 16, ____

4. 3, 3, 6, 5, 5, 10, 8, 8, 16, 13, 13, ____

5. 3, 5, 8, 12, 17, 23, ____

6. 0, 1, 2, 2, 3, 4, 5, 5, 6, 7, 8, 8, 9, 10, ____

7. 6, 36, 66, 96, ____

8. 1, 1, 1, 3, 2, 2, 2, 6, 5, 5, 5, 15, 14, 14, 14, ____

Two Kinds of Verbs: Action Verbs and State-of-Being Verbs.

Action verbs tell about an action you can see (<u>ran</u>) or an action you cannot see (<u>hear</u>).

State-of-being verbs tell what something or someone is (<u>is</u>, <u>are</u>, <u>am</u>, <u>appear</u>, <u>look</u>, etc.).

Make a design by coloring the action verbs orange and the state-of-being verbs green. Color the empty spaces any color you like, except orange or green.

			walk	has been			
			sound	call			
			dance	are			
			will be	sit			
	caught		laugh	been		honked	
			smell	plays			
see			wore	feel			seem
	being		will	gather		were	
		dive	jump	won	dive		
asking	rolled	wiggled	be	is	wiggled	read	eat
writing	cheer	buzzing	are	am	buzzing	barking	selling
		climbs	skiing	paint	cry		
	become		built	have been		was	
remain			has	carried			has had
			bake	felt			
	practice		became	blew		clapped	
			watched	wants			
			have	mopped			
			cooking	had			
			had been	hit			

Measuring with Metrics.

1 centimeter = 10 millimeters	1 meter = 10 decimeters
1 decimeter = 10 centimeters	1 meter = 100 centimeters
1 decimeter = 100 millimeters	1 meter = 1,000 millimeters

1 kilometer = 1,000 meters

cm 1 2 3 4 5 6 7 8 9 10 11 12 13 14 15

Estimate and then measure the following using the metric system. Use a metric ruler if you have one.

	Estimation	Measurement (Use more than one term of measurement.)
a book		
a toaster		
width of a drawer		
your little finger		
a can of soup		
a necklace		
a spatula		
an eraser		
the bathroom floor		
a garbage can		
a flashlight		
Choose things that you would like to measure.		

Do you remember that **g** and **c** both have a hard and soft sound? **G** as in su**g**ar (hard) and **g** as in **g**iant (soft), **c** as in **c**amel (hard) and **c** as in **c**ity (soft). In the first column of blanks, put **S** or **H** after each word to tell if the **c** or **g** is soft or hard. In the second column, match the hard or soft **c** and **g** words to the word or words that mean about the same.

EXAMPLE:

1. geyser	_____ H _____	in contact with	_____
2. music	_____	writing instrument	_____
3. advice	_____	produce	_____
4. generate	_____	adjust	_____
5. slogan	_____	operation	_____
6. cereal	_____	melody, harmony	_____
7. pencil	_____	violent contact	_____
8. regulate	_____	grain	_____
9. picture	_____	territory/land	_____
10. collide	_____	painting	_____
11. country	_____	hot spring	_____
12. gelatin	_____	motto	_____
15. surgery	_____	recommendation	_____
16. against	_____	jelly-like substance	_____

Sometimes people go to movies to escape reality. Can you think of some movies that are not realistic and some that are like real life? Which kinds of movies do you like best?

1. Write at least three movies under each column:

Realistic	**Not realistic**
_____	_____
_____	_____
_____	_____

2. Who is your favorite actor or actress? Why do you like this person?

_____

_____

Use the metric measure information on page 29 if you need help to do this activity.

Change each measurement to millimeters.

1. 25 cm

_____mm

2. 3 m

_____mm

3. 9 dm

_____mm

4. 10 dm

_____mm

5. 12 m

_____mm

Change each measurement to centimeters.

6. 8 m

_____cm

7. 50 mm

_____cm

8. 100 m

_____cm

9. 4 km

_____cm

10. 400 mm

_____cm

Use greater than (>), less than (<), and equal (=) signs.

11. 37 m ☐ 370 cm

12. 51 m ☐ 5 dm

13. 216 cm ☐ 216 mm

14. 40 cm ☐ 400 mm

15. 5 m ☐ 15 km

16. 80 km ☐ 80,000 m

What Time Is It?

1. What time was it 2 hours and 30 minutes earlier?

_____

2. What time was it 1 hour and 15 minutes earlier?

_____

3. What time will it be in 4 hours and 30 minutes?

_____

4. What time was it 3 hours and 45 minutes earlier?

_____

5. Kevin got to school at 8:25 a.m. He was 15 minutes late. What time did school start?

6. Stacy has 45 minutes left before the concert ends. It is 10:05 p.m. What time does the concert end?

7. Ruth left 35 minutes before her piano lesson that was at 9:45 a.m. What time did she leave?

8. Jasmine left the store at 10:15 a.m. and drove home in 25 minutes. What time did she arrive home?

The six sentences below tell the sequence of events in a story. They are in order. Write a story to go with them. Make sure the events in your story are in this order. Give your story a title. Write in cursive.

1. On Saturday, Mom and I went to a professional basketball game.
2. We rode the crowded subway to the game.
3. The Coliseum was even more crowded than the subway.
4. Mom and I traded seats because I couldn't see very well!
5. We both wanted our home team to win.
6. Because we were so tired after the game, we took a taxi home.

Title:

_____

_____

_____

_____

_____

_____

_____

_____

_____

_____

_____

_____

_____

_____

_____

_____

_____

_____

Vertical Flush

Can you figure out what makes water flow up into a glass in this experiment?

Stuff You Need:

adult
candle (short)
drinking glass (large)
food coloring
matches
pie tin
water

Parent Alert:

This experiment uses matches.
Make sure you supervise your child during this entire experiment!

Here's What to Do:

1. Put just enough water in the pie tin to cover the bottom so that there are no dry spots.

2. Put a few drops of food coloring in the water and swirl it around. If you do not have food coloring, the activity will still work. The food coloring just looks cool.

Always use extra caution when using matches or candles in experiments.

3. Place the candle in the middle of the pie tin and light it. Set the glass over the candle and see what happens.

What's This All About?

One way to change air pressure is to change the number of air molecules in a closed space. More molecules means higher pressure, and fewer molecules means lower pressure. Another way to change air pressure is to heat the molecules. Heated molecules move faster and whack into things harder. Cooler molecules move more slowly. Heating air up tends to increase air pressure; cooling it down tends to decrease air pressure.

When you set the glass over the burning candle, two things happen. First, the candle heats the air in the glass, which increases the air pressure by speeding up the molecules. Then, the flame takes oxygen out of the air, which changes the number of molecules and reduces the air pressure inside the glass. These two things cancel each other out, so nothing happens as long as the candle is burning.

When the candle goes out, no heat will be left to increase the air pressure in the glass. You will be left with low pressure inside because the flame has used up the oxygen molecules. The higher air pressure outside the glass then pushes the water up toward the lower air pressure inside the glass.

Charcoal Garden

Have you ever looked closely at ice crystals? How about salt crystals? Did you know that you can grow all kinds of crystals?

Stuff You Need:

ammonia   charcoal briquettes (4)
food coloring   laundry bluing
pie tin   salt
teaspoon   water

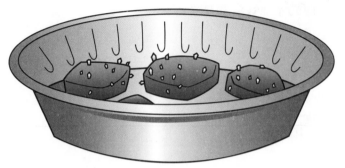

Here's What to Do:

1. Use the recipe listed below and mix up a batch of special solution:
   10 teaspoons water
   5 teaspoons salt
   5 teaspoons laundry bluing
   1 teaspoon ammonia

2. Arrange the charcoal pieces in the pie tin however you like. Pour the solution over the charcoal. There should be just enough solution in the pan to cover the bottom.

3. If you are using food coloring, drizzle it over the top of the pile of charcoal. If you do not use any, you will get white crystals with a blue tint.

4. Crystals will begin to form right away on the charcoal and also in the pan. As the solution evaporates, add more to the pan. If you pour the solution directly on the charcoal, the crystals (which are very fragile) will be crushed. Even blowing very hard on the crystals will knock them over.

What's This All About?

Charcoal is a porous material. It soaks up the liquid in the bottom of the pie tin and the liquid that is poured over the top. Once the mixture gets to the top of the charcoal, the liquid evaporates, leaving a crystal garden. The garden will continue to grow until the pie tin runs out of the solution or the crystals grow too tall to support their own weight and fall.

More Fun Ideas to Try:

Try using different substances to grow crystals. Copper sulfate may work in this experiment, too. Try naphthalene (mothballs) and alum. If you don't mind spending a little more money, silver nitrate makes a good batch of crystals. Any good book on crystals will list several more chemicals that can turn into crystals.

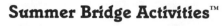

Motivational Calendar

Month

My parents and I decided that if I complete
20 days of **Summer Bridge Activities**™ and
read _____ minutes a day, my incentive/reward will be:

Child's Signature _____ Parent's Signature_____

Day 1	☆	📖	_____	**Day 11**	☆ 📖 _____
Day 2	☆	📖	_____	**Day 12**	☆ 📖 _____
Day 3	☆	📖	_____	**Day 13**	☆ 📖 _____
Day 4	☆	📖	_____	**Day 14**	☆ 📖 _____
Day 5	☆	📖	_____	**Day 15**	☆ 📖 _____
Day 6	☆	📖	_____	**Day 16**	☆ 📖 _____
Day 7	☆	📖	_____	**Day 17**	☆ 📖 _____
Day 8	☆	📖	_____	**Day 18**	☆ 📖 _____
Day 9	☆	📖	_____	**Day 19**	☆ 📖 _____
Day 10	☆	📖	_____	**Day 20**	☆ 📖 _____

Child: Color the ☆ for daily activities completed.
Color the 📖 for daily reading completed.

Parent: Initial the _____ when all activities are complete.

Discover Something New!

Fun Activity Ideas to Go Along with the Second Section!

1. Give your dog a bath or ask your neighbor or friend if you can give their dog a bath.

2. Pack a lunch and go to the park.

3. Roast marshmallows over a fire or BBQ.

4. Draw the shape of your state and put a star where you live. Draw your state flower, motto, and bird.

5. Write a poem that rhymes.

6. Make a batch of cookies and take them to a sick friend, neighbor, or relative.

7. Plant some flower or vegetable seeds in a pot and watch them grow.

8. Organize an earthquake drill for your family.

9. Get a piece of paper that is as long and as wide as you. Lie down on it and have someone outline you with a marker. Then color in the details—eyes, ears, mouth, clothes, arms, hands, etc.

10. Make a "Happy Birthday" card for a friend who is celebrating a birthday and give it to that person on his or her special day.

11. With bright colored markers, draw a picture of your favorite place to go. Paste it to a piece of posterboard and cut it into pieces for a jigsaw puzzle.

12. Make and fly a kite.

13. Invite your friends over for popcorn and vote on your favorite Disney movie. Watch the winning movie; then choose parts and act out the movie in your own way.

14. Read to younger children in your family or neighborhood.

15. Visit the library and attend story time.

16. Pick one of your favorite foods and learn how to make it.

17. Prepare a clean bed for your pet.

18. Get your neighborhood friends together and make a card of appreciation for the fire station closest to you. Then all of you deliver the card and take a tour of the station.

19. Invent a new game and play it with your friends.

20. Surprise a family member with breakfast in bed.

Negative and Positive Numbers.

A negative number has a quantity less than zero. A positive number, on the other hand, is a number greater than zero.

Illustrate and/or explain positive and negative numbers using a number line, a countdown at Cape Canaveral, or a thermometer.

Write a story problem to go with one of the illustrations and/or explanations you used above.

Facts from the Southern Colonies in the 1600s and 1700s.

From the list below, choose the word that means almost the same as the underlined word or phrase in the sentences.

| indigo | indentured servants | proprietor |
| slaves | cash crops | |

_____ 1. George Calvert was the first <u>owner</u> of a colony.

_____ 2. A lot of Southern farmers grew <u>crops that they could sell for money</u>.

_____ 3. In the 1740s, Eliza Lucas developed <u>a blue dye made from a plant</u>.

_____ 4. Originally, <u>people who agreed to work five or seven years to pay their passage to America</u> labored on Southern farms. These people were eventually replaced by <u>people captured from Africa who were forced to work for nothing</u>.

The New England Colonies. Circle the correct answer to complete each statement.

1. A person who wanted to purify the church was called a
   a. Programmer   **b.** Puritan   **c.** Convert
2. A person whose expertise is shipbuilding is called a
   a. carpenter   **b.** cartwright   **c.** shipwright
3. Usually in the center of town was a grassy area called a
   a. field   **b.** common   **c.** meadow

Word Meanings. Fill in the blanks from the word list below.

inland	escorts	allergy	impression	appalled
suspicious	conduct	knead	inlets	subscribe
desert	frank	margin	stethoscope	owing

1. All the _____ around the lake were crowded with boats.

2. Everyone in the class had a chance to listen to my heart through the _____.

3. The night watchman became _____ of the two men parked near the back door of the building.

4. We _____ to at least four different newspapers.

5. Did you leave a _____ on both sides of your paper?

6. Ted spends too much money. He is always _____ for something.

7. She was _____ in telling me she did not like my new dress.

8. Use both hands when you _____ the bread dough.

9. My _____ acts up every time I go to the mall because I'm allergic to perfume.

10. Toby's _____ at the party was rude and inexcusable.

Here is a list of words you should know how to spell.
Put the words in alphabetical order.

stranger	hurried	deciding	journey
toiletry	pottery	individual	adventure
subscription	reunite	robbery	identify
announcement	alleys	victorious	enemy
	celery	toil	

1. _____   7. _____   13. _____

2. _____   8. _____   14. _____

3. _____   9. _____   15. _____

4. _____   10. _____   16. _____

5. _____   11. _____   17. _____

6. _____   12. _____   18. _____

Deposits and Deductions.

Amanda opened a checking account on May 15th with $500.25. On May 31st she deposited another $496.80. On June 4th she withdrew $145.00 to buy a bicycle. On June 15th she deposited $435.20. On June 30th she deposited $600.00. On July 1st she withdrew $400.00 to go to Camp Rockland, plus she also needed $63.00 for a sleeping bag. On July 15th she deposited $110.00. On July 24th she withdrew $900.00 to buy a compact TV with a built-in VCR.

Use the chart below to record Amanda's checking account record.

DATE	DEPOSITED	WITHDREW	TOTAL $
May 15	$500.25		$500.25
May 31			
June 4			
June 15			
June 30			
July 1			
July 15			
July 24			

Remember: When you deposit money you add, and when you withdraw money you subtract.

Use Amanda's checking account record to graph the total dollar amounts.

	May 15	May 31	June 4	June 15	June 30	July 1	July 15	July 24
$2,000.00								
$1,800.00								
$1,600.00								
$1,400.00								
$1,200.00								
$1,000.00								
$800.00								
$600.00								
$500.00								
$400.00								

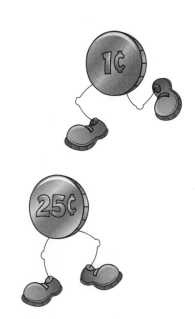

Underline the topic sentences of these paragraphs.

Remember: The topic sentence expresses the main idea of the paragraph.

1. The beginning of his life was very unusual. He was born in Texas into a large family. He fell out of a covered wagon and was not missed for many days because he had so many brothers and sisters. His parents couldn't find him, so he was raised by coyotes. He thought he was a coyote until he discovered he didn't have four feet and a tail.

2. Nuclear energy is the most awesome power that exists. It produces tremendous heat and light. It has been used to produce hydrogen and atomic bombs. It results from changes in the core of atoms. One important use of nuclear energy is in producing electricity. Scientists believe that if it were fully developed, nuclear energy could produce all the world's electricity for millions of years.

Now it's your turn! Write a topic sentence for these two paragraphs. Try to make it interesting so others will want to read the paragraph.

3. _____
They are among the world's oldest and largest living things. Some are thousands of years old and over 200 feet tall. Some of them are about 100 feet around at the base. You can see them in California and Oregon. They are the giant sequoia and redwood trees.

4. _____
It ranges from great works like Michelangelo's carvings to African masks. A piece of sculpture can be very large, like the Statue of Liberty, or small enough to sit on a table or hold in your hand. It has always played an important part in the history of man. Sculpture is an excellent way to express your own ideas and feelings.

Fill in the vowels for these spelling words. Then write each word two times in cursive.

1. r h _ n _ c _ r _ s   _____   _____

2. c h _ m _ c _ l   _____   _____

3. s t _ m _ c h   _____   _____

4. r h _ b _ r b   _____   _____

5. s c h _ l _ s t _ c   _____   _____

6. r h _ t h m   _____   _____

7. l _ g g _ g _   _____   _____

8. r _ m _ _ n d _ r   _____   _____

Remember: When talking about fractions, the denominator names the number of equal parts of a whole amount, and the numerator names the number of parts being taken from the whole.

Day 3

Write the fraction that tells what part is shaded.

1.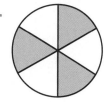

2.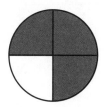

3.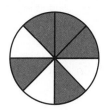

4.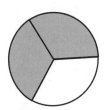

_____ _____ _____ _____

5.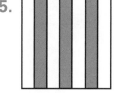

6.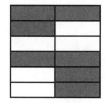

7.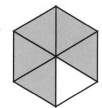

8.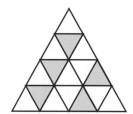

_____ _____ _____ _____

Write each fraction on the number line.

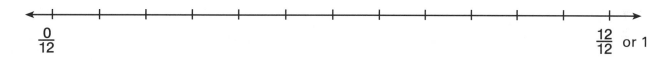

$\frac{0}{12}$ $\frac{12}{12}$ or 1

9. $\frac{3}{12}$ 10. $\frac{7}{12}$ 11. $\frac{10}{12}$ 12. $\frac{1}{12}$ 13. $\frac{5}{12}$ 14. $\frac{9}{12}$

Use < (less than), > (greater than), and = (equal to) to compare these fractions.

15. $\frac{7}{15}$ ☐ $\frac{9}{15}$ 16. $\frac{3}{4}$ ☐ $\frac{6}{8}$ 17. $\frac{4}{6}$ ☐ $\frac{1}{3}$

18. $\frac{5}{9}$ ☐ $\frac{5}{8}$ 19. $\frac{7}{8}$ ☐ $\frac{14}{16}$ 20. $\frac{9}{9}$ ☐ $\frac{8}{8}$

21. $\frac{1}{10}$ ☐ $\frac{1}{5}$ 22. $\frac{14}{20}$ ☐ $\frac{9}{10}$ 23. $\frac{6}{12}$ ☐ $\frac{1}{2}$

Read a book or story of your choice and do the following.

1. Write the names of three characters and tell why they were important to the story.

   a. _____

   b. _____

   c. _____

2. What are some important details or events from the story you read? List at least four.

   a. _____

   b. _____

   c. _____

   d. _____

3. How did the story end?

4. Would you like it to end differently? If so, how would you have it end?

Circle the seven major plates of the earth's surface in the list. On the world map below, divide the earth into the seven plates. See if you can label them correctly. Check the answers in the back to see how close you came!

Alaska
North America
Australia-India
China
Atlantic
Arctic
Eurasia
Pacific
North Pole
South America
Japan
India
African
Canada-USA
Antarctic
Western

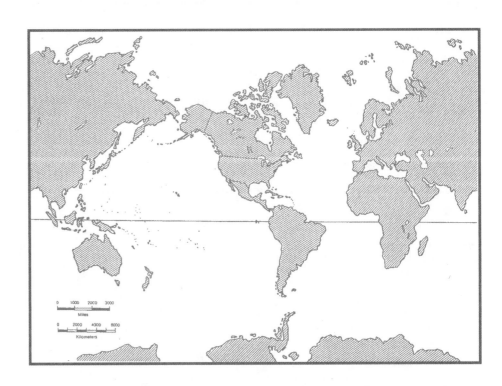

Divide to find the fraction of a number.

1. $\frac{1}{2}$ of 10 = ____   2. $\frac{1}{8}$ of 24 = ____   3. $\frac{1}{6}$ of 48 = ____   4. $\frac{1}{5}$ of 45 = ____

5. $\frac{1}{4}$ of 32 = ____   6. $\frac{1}{3}$ of 60 = ____   7. $\frac{1}{7}$ of 56 = ____   8. $\frac{1}{12}$ of 36 = ____

Find the equivalent fractions.

9. $\frac{3}{4} = \frac{}{8}$ 10. $\frac{5}{8} = \frac{}{16}$ 11. $\frac{10}{25} = \frac{2}{}$ 12. $\frac{4}{9} = \frac{}{36}$

13. $\frac{7}{12} = \frac{28}{}$ 14. $\frac{6}{6} = \frac{12}{}$ 15. $\frac{3}{4} = \frac{}{20}$ 16. $\frac{7}{15} = \frac{}{45}$

Find the equivalent fractions.

17. $\frac{9}{12} = \frac{36}{}$ 18. $\frac{2}{3} = \frac{10}{}$ 19. $\frac{3}{10} = \frac{18}{}$ 20. $\frac{1}{3} = \frac{3}{}$

21. $\frac{5}{8} = \frac{}{72}$ 22. $\frac{2}{5} = \frac{8}{}$ 23. $\frac{5}{12} = \frac{}{36}$ 24. $\frac{11}{24} = \frac{44}{}$

Reduce the fractions to the lowest terms that make whole or mixed numbers.

25. $\frac{56}{6} =$ 26. $\frac{14}{4} =$ 27. $\frac{38}{8} =$ 28. $\frac{51}{8} =$

29. $\frac{17}{2} =$ 30. $\frac{35}{5} =$ 31. $\frac{14}{6} =$ 32. $\frac{10}{8} =$

Health—Communicable Diseases. Answer T for true or F for false to the following statements. If false, correct the sentence so it is true.

____ 1. Pathogens are people who build roads.

____ 2. Communicable diseases are spread by contact with an infected person.

____ 3. The common cold, flu, and sore throat are considered communicable diseases.

____ 4. Pathogens cannot spread by touch or through the air.

____ 5. Washing hands does not reduce the risk of pathogens entering the body.

Imagine you are principal of your school. As principal, you must write some rules that would help the school be free from the spread of pathogens that can cause communicable diseases. Write three rules you would enforce.

Main Verbs and Helping Verbs. Remember: The verb in a sentence may be one word or a few words. Some words can be either a helping verb or a main verb. Underline the complete verb in these sentences.

EXAMPLE: Jack <u>was</u> in town. Or, Jack <u>was working</u> in town.

1. Joseph is walking to the park with his friends.

2. My mother has been working at Sears for many years.

3. I might have called if I had known you were home.

4. The snowstorm yesterday buried all the beautiful flowers.

5. Jim does enjoy sports.

6. Mark is playing outdoors with Sam.

7. David does his homework every day.

8. Misty and Courtney are watching television.

●●●●●●●●●●●●●●●●●●●●●●●●●●●●●●●●●●●

Below are some sentences about our first president, George Washington. Read the sentences and put them in the correct chronological order.

____ When his father died in 1743, Washington went to live on a plantation known as Mount Vernon.

____ George Washington was born in 1732 in Virginia.

____ Washington married Martha Dandridge Custis in 1759.

____ Washington was elected first president of the United States in 1789.

____ George Washington died in 1799.

____ In 1758 Washington became a member of the Virginia House of Burgesses.

____ Beginning his military career at age 21, Washington served in the French and Indian War from 1754–1758.

____ During the Revolutionary War, Washington won victories at Trenton in 1776 and Yorktown in 1778.

____ Washington believed America needed independence from England. In 1778, he was chosen to lead the Continental Army against the British soldiers.

"Washington" is the name of our nation's capital, a state, thirty-one counties, and at least sixteen cities. Why do you think so many places are named after George Washington?

●●●●●●●●●●●●●●●●●●●●●●●●●●●●●●●●●●

Estimate first; then solve the problem to see how close you came.

EXAMPLE:

		Est.					
1.	6,525	7,000	**2.**	1,236	**3.**	74,652
	3,910	4,000		4,253		75,843
	+2,335	2,000		+7,237		+18,284
actual	12,770			____		____
estimate	13,000	13,000		____		____

4.	365,244	**5.**	866,533	**6.**	904,568
	−79,087		−278,184		−578,179
actual	____		____		____
estimate	____		____		____

7.	533	**8.**	975	**9.**	4,675
	× 24		× 53		× 85
actual	____		____		____
estimate	____		____		____

10.	24)164	**11.**	80)286	**12.**	62)190
actual	____		____		____
estimate	____		____		____

Give the integer for each letter on the number line.

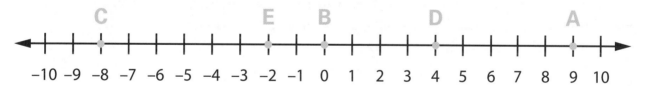

1. A = _____   **2.** B = _____   **3.** C = _____   **4.** D = _____   **5.** E = _____

Use <, >, or = for each ◯.

1. ⁻8 ◯ 8   **2.** 0 ◯ ⁻3

3. 15 ◯ ⁻16   **4.** ⁻4 ◯ 4

5. ⁻12 ◯ ⁻20   **6.** ⁻3 ◯ ⁻4

Write your telephone number down the side of the paper. Include your area code. For each digit, write a word that has that number of syllables. Look in the dictionary for help. If you have numerals over 5 you can use two words to total the number. If your phone number has a zero, leave the line blank.

_____   _____

_____   _____

_____   _____

_____   _____

_____   _____

_____   _____

_____   _____

_____   _____

The following words are names of birds. Some are water birds, some are land birds, and some are tropical birds. Some can't even fly!

If you want to be a bird-watcher, you will need to know the names of birds. Unscramble these words, and you will be on your way! The first letter is underlined.

1. aayr<u>c</u>n   _____

2. wii<u>k</u>   _____

3. dirnaal<u>c</u>   _____

4. eon<u>hr</u>   _____

5. un<u>p</u>iegn   _____

6. <u>h</u>bdrmuimgni   _____

7. ono<u>l</u>   _____

8. idn<u>m</u>cgkriob   _____

9. nacuo<u>t</u>   _____

10. ic<u>o</u>srht   _____

11. prwora<u>s</u>   _____

12. n<u>f</u>oacl   _____

13. tsnaha<u>p</u>e   _____

14. <u>p</u>eatreak   _____

15. g<u>e</u>ela   _____

16. maio<u>f</u>gln   _____

Grocery Store Estimation in Weight and Cost.

Before you go to the grocery store, estimate how much you think certain produce will weigh. Make a chart showing your estimates; then go to the grocery store and actually weigh the produce. Chart these results. <u>Remember</u>: Most scales in the United States will be in pounds and ounces, whereas other countries use grams and kilograms.

EXAMPLE:

produce	estimated weight	actual weight	estimated cost	actual cost
6 apples	3 pounds	2 pounds 3 oz	$3.00	$3.15

Precursors to the Revolutionary War. Answer the following questions. Use the time line.

1754 French and Indian War	1763 King George III gives proclamation to limit western settlement	1765 Stamp Act	1770 Boston Massacre	1773 Boston Tea Party	1774 Intolerable Acts	1775 Battles fought at Lexington and Concord

1. How many years after the French and Indian War did the Boston Massacre occur? ____

2. Which events occurred in Boston? _____, _____

3. Which occurred first—the Stamp Act or the Intolerable Acts? How many years are there between these events? _____, _____

4. Choose four events on the time line. Draw and color four pictures in the rectangles below that show the sequence of those events.

Circle the correct form of the <u>be</u> verb.

1. I (be, am) guessing the number of pennies in the jar.
2. What (is, be) your favorite month of the year?
3. The workmen (been, were) repairing the road in front of our house.
4. Carla (was, were) laughing very loud.
5. (Is, Are) you the team leader?
6. My Uncle Clint (been, has been, have been) an astronaut and is now a teacher.
7. The haunted house (is being, are being) torn down.
8. We (be, will be) playing in the orchestra on Saturday night.

Now write a sentence for each of these words.
Make sure your sentences are different from the ones above.

9. were _____

10. has been _____

11. was being _____

12. are _____

Match the type of plate boundary with the correct synonyms and definitions.

Synonyms	Definitions
1. sliding	a. plates push against each other
2. spreading	b. plates move away from each other
3. colliding	c. plates slide by each other

Synonyms	Definitions	Type of Plate Boundary
_____	_____	divergent boundary
_____	_____	convergent boundary
_____	_____	transform boundary

Determine which picture below represents each type of plate boundary listed above.

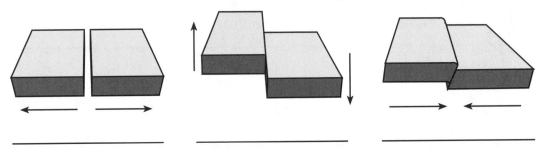

_____ _____ _____

Match the geometric terms with their definitions.

_____ segment

_____ ray

_____ angles

_____ perpendicular lines

_____ parallel lines

_____ congruent

_____ symmetric

_____ congruent segments

_____ circumference

_____ radius

_____ diameter

_____ AB or BA

a. lines that never meet

b. rays with the same endpoint

c. a figure that can be folded and both parts fit perfectly

d. has an end point or a starting point and can go from there in one direction

e. a part of a line that can be named by its endpoints

f. lines that intersect to form right angles of 90 degrees

g. ways of labeling endpoints on a segment

h. figures having the same shape and size

i. segment that passes through the center of a circle and has both endpoints on the circle

j. a line connecting the center of a circle to a point on the outside of a circle

k. the distance around a circle

l. have equal lengths

Illustrate each of these geometric terms.

1. segment

2. parallel lines

3. circumference

4. ray

5. congruent

6. radius

7. angle

8. symmetric

9. diameter

10. perpendicular lines

11. congruent segments

12. AB or BA

Read this part of the Declaration of Independence and answer the questions below.

> We hold these truths to be self-evident, that all men are created equal, that they are endowed by their Creator with certain unalienable Rights, that among these are Life, Liberty and the pursuit of Happiness.
>
> That to secure these rights, Governments are instituted among Men, deriving their just powers from the consent of the governed.
>
> That whenever any Form of Government becomes destructive of these ends, it is the Right of the People to alter or to abolish it, and to institute new Government, laying its foundation on such principles and organizing its powers in such form, as to them shall seem most likely to effect their Safety and Happiness.

1. What are the basic rights of all people according to the Declaration of Independence?

2. Why are governments "instituted," or created?

3. What should people do if they feel the government is not acting in their best interest?

4. Draw and color a flag that expresses the feelings and beliefs of the Declaration of Independence.

Earth's Magnetic Field. Read the following passage and answer the questions below.

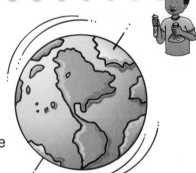

The earth is like a huge magnet. It has a magnetic field. Its magnetism is the strongest at the North and South Poles. When rock forms, any magnetic particles will align themselves with the earth's magnetic field. They will point toward either the North or South Poles. There are some rocks that do not point to the current North and South Poles. Scientists conclude that either the North and South Poles have moved, or the rocks themselves have moved since they were formed. Most feel the rocks and continents have moved. Geologists use this information to determine how the continents have moved over time.

1. Why is the earth compared to a magnet?

2. Where are the earth's strongest points of magnetism?

3. How can geologists study the movements of the continents?

4. What would happen to a ship and its compass if the earth's magnetic strong area became the western part of the earth and NOT the North Pole?

Find the Perimeter.

Remember: To find the perimeter, you have to add the lengths of each side.

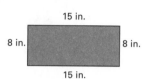

15 in. · 8 in. · 8 in. · 15 in.

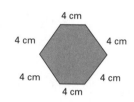

4 cm · 4 cm · 4 cm · 4 cm · 4 cm · 4 cm

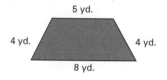

5 yd. · 4 yd. · 4 yd. · 8 yd.

1. _____ inches

2. _____ centimeters

3. _____ yards

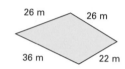

26 m · 26 m · 36 m · 22 m

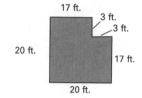

17 ft. · 3 ft. · 3 ft. · 20 ft. · 17 ft. · 20 ft.

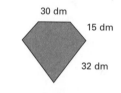

30 dm · 15 dm · 32 dm

4. _____ meters

5. _____ feet

6. _____ decimeters

Find the Area.

Remember: Area is measured in square units. Area = length × width.

Remember: Area = $\frac{1}{2}$ × base × height for triangles

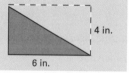

4 in. · 6 in.

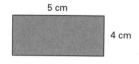

5 cm · 4 cm

8 yd · 8 yd

12 in. · 36 in.

7. _____ cm² (square centimeters)

8. _____ square yards

9. _____ square inches

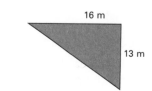

4 in. · 6 in.

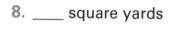

16 m · 13 m

70 dm · 24 dm

10. _____ square inches

11. _____ m²

12. _____ dm²

Many earthquakes occur at the plate boundaries. Study the following map of earthquake epicenters and answer the questions below.

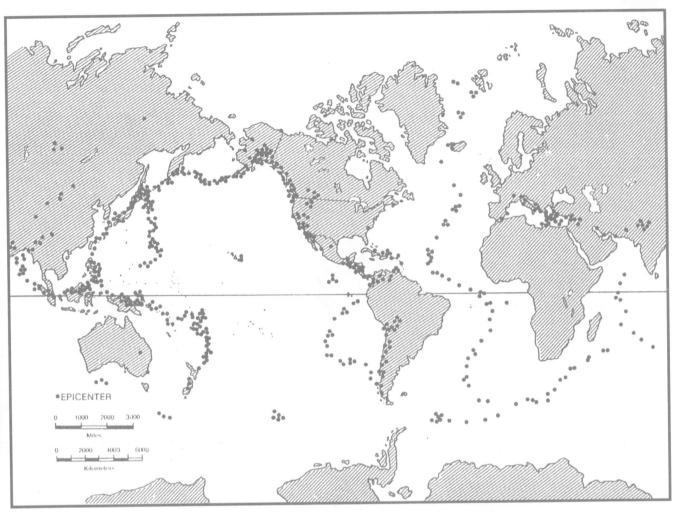

1. Color the areas with the most earthquake activity. What pattern do you see?

2. Review the map on plate boundaries on page 42. What is similar about these boundaries and earthquake activity?

3. Explain how you came up with your answer for question 2.

4. Observe the earthquakes that occur in the interior of the plates (e.g., China, U.S., and Australia). How is the distribution of these earthquakes different from that of earthquakes along the plate boundaries?

Write the rest of the number families.

1. 78 × 42 = 3,276

    42 × 78 = 3,276

    3,276 ÷ 42 = 78

    3,276 ÷ 78 = 42

2. 39 × 56 = 2,184

    _____

    _____

    _____

3. 95 × 37 = 3,515

    _____

    _____

    _____

4. 49 × 76 =

    _____

    _____

5. 141 × 27 =

    _____

    _____

6. 3,762 ÷ 38 =

    _____

    _____

7. 26,320 ÷ 47 =

    _____

    _____

8. 48,306 ÷ 83 =

    _____

    _____

9. 194 × 92 =

    _____

    _____

10. 16,019 ÷ 83 =

    _____

    _____

11. 2,650 × 54 =

    _____

    _____

12. 876,600 ÷ 360 =

    _____

    _____

There are a lot of ways you can take care of your respiratory system. Some ways are exercising regularly, not smoking, and not inhaling chemicals produced by products such as paint or glue. Look at some old magazines and ask your parents if you can cut out pictures of people caring for their respiratory system. If you don't have any old magazines, draw and color pictures.

Read these paragraphs. Draw a line through the sentence or sentences that do not belong in the paragraph. Tell why.

Remember to ask yourself:

1. **Does the paragraph have one main idea?**
2. **Do all the sentences in the paragraph tell about the main idea?**
3. **Is every sentence in the paragraph a complete sentence?**

1. Water in the ocean never stops moving. The most well-known movements are waves. Waves are set in motion by earthquakes, winds, and the gravitational pull of the sun and moon. Ocean water is also very salty. On shore, we see waves caused by the wind. Their size depends on whether they come from far across the ocean or are caused by winds from nearby storms.

2. The beaver is a furry animal with a flat, wide tail that looks like a paddle. There are more beavers in the U.S. and Canada than anywhere else. The beaver's strong front teeth are used for cutting down trees. They use the branches to build dams and homes, but they eat the bark from them first. Beavers almost always seem. We often call people who work hard "eager beavers."

3. Write a paragraph. Try to remember the three rules as you write.

Earthquakes. Fill in the blanks in the paragraph with the words listed.

seismologists	seismic waves	fault	focus
earthquake	energy	above	beneath
	epicenter	fracture	

An _____ is sudden shaking of the ground that happens when _____

stored in rock is released. A _____ is a break, or _____, in the earth's

crust. As rock breaks, stored energy moves along the fault. The hypocenter, or _____,

is where an earthquake begins. This occurs _____ the earth's surface. The point

on the earth's crust which is directly _____ the focus is called the _____.

_____, or shock waves, move out from the focus and cause the ground to

shake. _____ study and record these shock waves and determine the size of the

earthquake.

In 1617, John Napier used a method of multiplying with rods marked with numbers. Some people call it "Napier's Bones" or "lattice" multiplication. When placing the appropriate "bones" side by side, you read the product of multiplication.

EXAMPLE: 528 × 347 = _183,216_

Build your "lattice" by multiplying the individual digits of the factors you are multiplying. Start from the top left corner of the chart each time. For the example problem, go 5 over and 3 down on the big chart to get $\frac{1}{5}$. Then, go 2 over and 3 down to find $\frac{0}{6}$, etc. Starting in the lower right corner, add along the diagonals (indicated by the arrows in the example below), carrying the remainder to the next diagonal.

	1	2	3	4	5	6	7	8	9
1	0/1	0/2	0/3	0/4	0/5	0/6	0/7	0/8	0/9
2	0/2	0/4	0/6	0/8	1/0	1/2	1/4	1/6	1/8
3	0/3	0/6	0/9	1/2	1/5	1/8	2/1	2/4	2/7
4	0/4	0/8	1/2	1/6	2/0	2/4	2/8	3/2	3/6
5	0/5	1/0	1/5	2/0	2/5	3/0	3/5	4/0	4/5
6	0/6	1/2	1/8	2/4	3/0	3/6	4/2	4/8	5/4
7	0/7	1/4	2/1	2/8	3/5	4/2	4/9	5/6	6/3
8	0/8	1/6	2/4	3/2	4/0	4/8	5/6	6/4	7/2
9	0/9	1/8	2/7	3/6	4/5	5/4	6/3	7/2	8/1

Lattice example for 528 × 347:

5	2	8	×
1/5	0/6	2/4	3
2/0	0/8	3/2	4
3/5	1/4	5/6	7

Result: 1 8 3, 2 1 6

1. 476 × 304 = _____

2. 722 × 436 = _____

3. 821 × 569 = _____

4. 835 × 321 = _____

5. 605 × 843 = _____

6. 349 × 275 = _____

Some key words and punctuation marks signal that an author is giving a context clue. These include dashes, commas, parentheses, and phrases like <u>which is</u>, <u>in other words</u>, <u>for instance</u>, and <u>etc</u>. In these sentences write what the underlined words mean. Then write the key words or punctuation marks that helped you tell the word's meaning.

EXAMPLE: The candidate shouted through a <u>megaphone</u> (large funnel-shaped horn) so the crowd could hear him.

megaphone _____*Large funnel-shaped horn*_____ *parentheses*

1. I feel <u>torpid</u>—sluggish and lazy—in the hot summer weather.

   torpid _____

2. Paul Bunyan used an <u>adze</u>, which is a flat-bladed ax, to cut down the forest.

   adze_____

3. The cook made <u>ragout</u>, a highly seasoned stew, every day for the ranch hands.

   ragout_____

4. Jason mashed his <u>patella</u>, in other words, his kneecap.

   patella_____

5. David can play a <u>marimba</u> (a xylophone).

   marimba _____

Write your own sentences using a word many people would not know. Use context clues in each one.

6. _____

7. _____

● ●

Add a prefix or a suffix to the following base words. Choose six of the words you made and write sentences with them.

1. ____agree
2. ____placed
3. ____respect____
4. ____capable
5. avoid____
6. ____change
7. delay____
8. ____number____
9. loyal____
10. hazard____
11. care____
12. ____depend____
13. ____necessary
14. smart____
15. thought____
16. marvel____
17. ____verb
18. ____mature
19. ____comfort____
20. ____plant
21. act____

● ●

Mixed Practice. Find the missing factors.

1. 67 × _____ = 536

2. 96 × _____ = 864

3. _____ × 77 = 385

4. _____ × 84 = 924

5. 2,210 ÷ _____ = 85

6. 5,518 ÷ _____ = 62

7. 29 × _____ = 1,972

8. 19,347 − _____ = 18,470

9. 23,432 + _____ = 24,089

10. 32 × _____ = 6,400

11. _____ × 75 = 11,250

12. 4,905 ÷ _____ = 327

13. 56,993 − _____ = 55,598

14. 4,266 ÷ _____ = 711

15. 33 × _____ = 17,886

16. _____ + 34,561 = 40,090

17. 307 × _____ = 18,113

18. 741 × _____ = 61,503

19. 50,000 ÷ _____ = 1,250

20. _____ × 56 = 16,016

21. 40,572 ÷ _____ = 126

22. 19,263 + _____ = 66,390

23. 73,477 − _____ = 62,305

24. _____ − 80,399 = 110,099

The Revolutionary War. Answer <u>T</u> for true or <u>F</u> for false to the following statements. If false, correct the statement so it will be true.

_____ 1. Loyalists supported the colonists.

_____ 2. Thomas Paine convinced many colonists to break from Great Britain with his pamphlet <u>Common Sense</u>.

_____ 3. The British had no struggle in taking Breed's Hill, known as the Battle of Bunker Hill.

_____ 4. The Declaration of Independence was written by John Adams on July 4, 1775.

_____ 5. The patriots had support from many American women when fighting their battles.

_____ 6. Mary Ludwig Hays, known as Molly Pitcher, carried pitchers of water to men who were fighting in battles.

57

Irregular Verbs. Change the present form of the verb at the first of the sentence to the past form. Write the past form in the blank.

EXAMPLE:

wear   I ___*wore*___ an old coat to school.

ring   **1.** The telephone _____ ten times before she answered it.

build   **2.** The contractor _____ a new apartment building every year.

feed   **3.** Aunt Dawn _____ her cats three times a day.

choose   **4.** We each _____ a friend to go with us to Disneyland.

spend   **5.** My brother _____ all of his allowance on ice cream.

spin   **6.** The top _____ for five minutes.

run   **7.** Our family _____ in a marathon two summers ago.

eat   **8.** The monkey _____ four bananas.

shake   **9.** I was so afraid of the dark that I _____ when the lights went out.

hold   **10.** Kit _____ his breath for one minute.

bleed   **11.** My nose _____ for half an hour last night.

draw   **12.** The class _____ pictures showing what they did on their field trip.

ride   **13.** Alexander _____ his Shetland pony in the rodeo parade last summer.

teach   **14.** Julie's mother _____ us how to jump double Dutch.

fight   **15.** My sisters and I _____ a lot when we were children.

Quotes.

Make a list of favorite or frequently used quotes among your family and friends. Have your family and friends help you compile your list.

EXAMPLE: *If wishes were fishes we'd all take a swim.*

Simplify the fractions down to the <u>lowest term possible</u>.

EXAMPLE:

1. $\frac{5}{10} = \frac{1}{2}$

2. $\frac{8}{12} = $ ___

3. $\frac{6}{9} = $ ___

4. $\frac{15}{25} = $ ___

5. $\frac{50}{75} = $ ___

6. $\frac{16}{20} = $ ___

7. $\frac{9}{72} = $ ___

8. $\frac{18}{45} = $ ___

9. $\frac{24}{32} = $ ___

10. $\frac{75}{100} = $ ___

11. $\frac{36}{45} = $ ___

12. $\frac{16}{24} = $ ___

13. $\frac{10}{35} = $ ___

14. $\frac{4}{18} = $ ___

15. $\frac{9}{15} = $ ___

16. $\frac{14}{21} = $ ___

17. $\frac{150}{200} = $ ___

18. $\frac{32}{40} = $ ___

19. $\frac{81}{135} = $ ___

20. $\frac{280}{420} = $ ___

Heroes in America. Match these people with the important contributions they made during America's fight for independence.

____ George Washington

____ Thomas Jefferson

____ Patrick Henry

____ Benjamin Franklin

____ Thomas Paine

____ John Paul Jones

____ Mary Ludwig Hays

____ Francis Marion

____ Deborah Sampson

a. "Swamp Fox," guerrilla warfare

b. commander of American ship *Bonhomme Richard*

c. dressed in men's clothing and joined the army

d. crossed the Delaware River on Christmas Eve

e. "Gentlemen, we must all hang together, or most assuredly we shall all hang separately."

f. carried pitchers of water to soldiers

g. "Give me liberty or give me death!"

h. <u>Common Sense</u>

i. wrote the Declaration of Independence

Choose one of these people and do a small report on him/her. After giving so much of themselves to gain independence for America, how do you think they would feel if they saw America today? What do you think they would say?

Direct objects are nouns or pronouns that complete or receive the action of the verb. They follow action verbs only. Circle the verb and underline the direct object in these sentences. Use the direct objects to complete the puzzle.

EXAMPLE:

1. John Smith (guided) the <u>colonists</u> in the new world.

2. The robber threw the jewels into the bag.

3. Sarah bought some groceries at the supermarket.

4. The crowd begged the musicians to play more.

5. We captured the tarantula in an old glass jar.

6. The sun melted the icicles on the house.

7. My brother, the quarterback, made a touchdown.

8. The movers loaded the furniture into the truck.

9. Loryn watches movies with her friends.

10. Trenton sold fifty tickets for the drawing.

11. Julia cut the watermelon into a dozen pieces.

12. The tangled string ruined my kite.

13. Rosa borrowed my new umbrella.

Complete the puzzle.

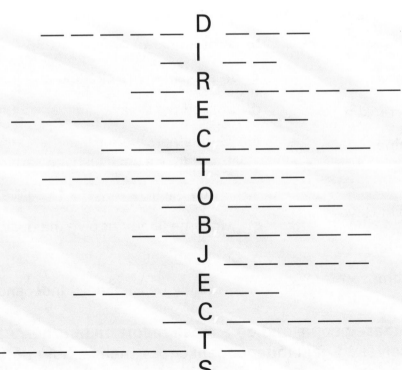

Mysterious Division Power. Choose any 2-digit number. Write it 3 times to make a 6-digit number. Divide it by 13; then divide the answer by 21, and divide that answer by 37.

EXAMPLE:

<u>14</u> 141,414 ÷ 13 = _10,878_ ÷ 21 = _518_ ÷ 37 = _14_ **MAGIC!**

1. <u>56</u> 565,656 ÷ 13 = _____ ÷ 21 = ___ ÷ 37 = ___

2. <u>35</u> 353,535 ÷ 13 = _____ ÷ 21 = ___ ÷ 37 = ___

3. <u>73</u> 737,373 ÷ 13 = _____ ÷ 21 = ___ ÷ 37 = ___

4. <u>29</u> 292,929 ÷ 13 = _____ ÷ 21 = ___ ÷ 37 = ___

Now use your own 2-digit numbers.

5. ____ _____ ÷ 13 = _____ ÷ 21 = ___ ÷ 37 = ___

6. ____ _____ ÷ 13 = _____ ÷ 21 = ___ ÷ 37 = ___

7. ____ _____ ÷ 13 = _____ ÷ 21 = ___ ÷ 37 = ___

8. ____ _____ ÷ 13 = _____ ÷ 21 = ___ ÷ 37 = ___

Teeth. Match the appropriate term and definition.

____ crown

____ enamel

____ dentin

____ pulp

____ cementum

____ root

a. hard tissue that covers the crown of tooth

b. part of tooth above the gum

c. hard tissue that covers the root

d. part of tooth that holds it in the jawbone

e. hard tissue that forms body of tooth

f. soft tissue that contains nerves and blood vessels in center of tooth

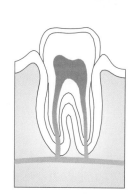

Write a short story titled "The Tale of Tooth City." Have a villain whose name might be "Wicked Wizard Plaque." Be creative with your story. Have a happy ending with healthy teeth.

_____

_____

_____

_____

Read these sentences; then write the underlined word on the line, leaving a space between the syllables. Use the dictionary if you need help.

1. We used some old <u>wicker</u> chairs on our patio. _____

2. <u>Lavender</u> is a shade of the color purple. _____

3. My brother, who is six feet six inches tall, has <u>enormous</u> feet. _____

4. In the spring, my favorite flowering bush is the <u>lilac</u>. _____

5. We use <u>natural</u> gas to heat our house. _____

6. I could hear a <u>whispering</u> voice behind me. _____

7. Have you ever been to <u>San Francisco</u>? _____

8. The <u>coauthor</u> of my new book is Carla Powers. _____

9. We think it's fun to visit cities that have <u>cobblestone</u> streets. _____

10. How old were you when you learned the <u>alphabet</u>? _____

11. Allen acted like a <u>zombie</u> after being up all night. _____

12. The comedian's <u>originality</u> was amusing. _____

Analogies are similar relationships between two pairs of words. Write an analogy to finish each sentence.

EXAMPLE:

1. <u>Tree</u> is to <u>lumber</u> as <u>wheat</u> is to ___*flour*___.

2. <u>Bricks</u> are to a <u>wall</u> as <u>fingers</u> are to _____.

3. <u>Page</u> is to <u>book</u> as _____ is to the <u>United States</u>.

4. <u>Finger</u> is to <u>hand</u> as <u>toe</u> is to _____.

5. <u>Brake</u> is to <u>stop</u> as <u>engine</u> is to _____.

6. <u>Penny</u> is to <u>dime</u> as <u>inch</u> is to _____.

7. <u>Mechanic</u> is to <u>motors</u> as <u>plumber</u> is to _____.

8. <u>Space</u> is to <u>rocket</u> as _____ is to <u>boat</u>.

9. <u>Bird</u> is to <u>nest</u> as _____ is to <u>den</u>.

10. <u>Stage</u> is to <u>actor</u> as <u>pit</u> is to _____.

Chart the graph point by point. The first number tells how far to go to the right. The second number tells how far to move up. The distance between the grid lines represents 2 units.

1. Place the dot and letter on the point called for. The first one is done for you.

(2, 2) dot A
(12, 16) dot H
(16, 12) dot J
(6, 4) dot P
(14, 10) dot K
(10, 14) dot G
(4, 6) dot B
(8, 12) dot F
(8, 6) dot O
(12, 8) dot L
(8, 10) dot D
(10, 8) dot N
(13, 13) dot I
(6, 8) dot C
(10, 11) dot E
(11, 10) dot M
(16, 4) draw a ☆
(4, 14) draw a ☆
(2, 18) draw a ☆
(16, 8) draw a ●
(2, 10) draw a ●
(10, 18) draw a ●

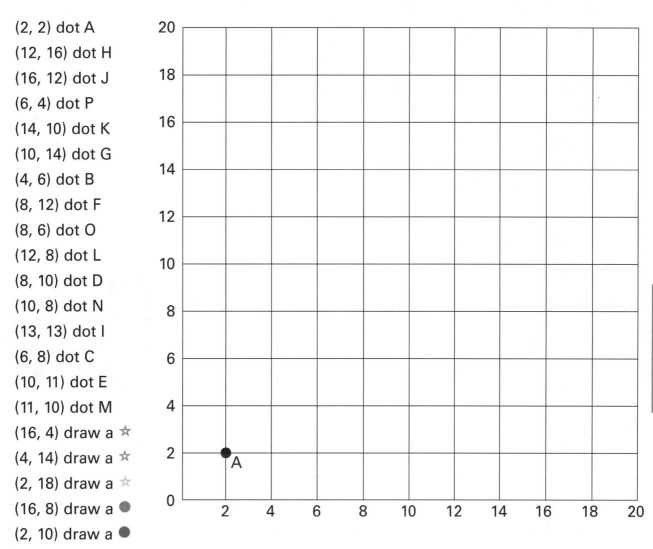

2. Connect dots A through P in alphabetical order.

3. Connect dot P to A.

4. Connect dots E to I and I to M.

Make a "point by point" direction course and have a friend or family member see if they can graph it. You could make a design, picture, or map. Use your imagination and have fun.

Circle the correct noun.

1. The (Farmers', Farmers) Market was only open on Friday.

2. That (mountain, mountains) peak is too hard for me to climb.

3. (Ed White's, Ed White) was the first astronaut to walk in space.

4. We saw a herd of (deer, deers) along the side of the road.

5. Why do (goose, geese) have webbed (foot, feet)?

Write the plural form of each noun to fill in the blanks.

potato
man
trout
party
elf

6. The _____ on our farm were the best!

7. The nurse took the pulses of the _____.

8. My father caught ten rainbow _____ that day.

9. The _____ we went to were all fun.

10. Many _____ worked on the shoes for the queen.

Fill in the blanks with proper nouns.

11. We live very close to the _____ Mountains.

12. _____ comes in the month of October.

13. The _____ Islands are very beautiful.

14. Judge _____ went on vacation as soon as the trial was over.

15. _____ favorite basketball team is the _____.

Fill in the blanks. Writing is a process of steps.

Step one:	Prewriting should include these activities: _____ ideas that you want to write about, _____ a topic, _____ ideas, and _____ ideas.
Step two:	Write some paragraphs about your topic.
Step three:	Kinds of information you can include about the topic are _____, _____, _____, _____, _____, and _____.
Step four:	Describe things about the topic in the _____ order.
Step five:	Proofread and check for mistakes in _____, _____, and _____.
Step six:	Rewrite and _____.

Exchange and Share $906.00. You have $906.00 to share among 7 family members. Find out if you can share it equally. To begin with, you have nine $100 bills, no $10 bills, and six $1 bills. Share and exchange down.

1. You have nine $100 bills. How many $100 bills does each family member get?_____ How many are left? _____

2. Exchange the $100 bills you have left for _____ $10 bills.

3. Each family member gets _____ $10 bills. How many are left? _____

4. Exchange your $10 bills for _____ $1 bills. How many $1 bills do you have? _____

5. Each family member gets _____ $1 bills. How many are left? _____

6. Each family member gets _____ $100 bills, _____ $10 bills, and _____ $1 bills.

7. How much money does each family member get? _____

8. What could you do with the amount left over? _____

9. Is there another way to share the money equally? _____ Show us!

Make up your own "Exchange and Share" situation or use the following: $504 among 21 people. Use the above method.

The Bill of Rights are the first ten amendments added to the Constitution. Other amendments also have been added. Read the passages below and determine which situations are constitutional or unconstitutional. Then write down which amendment would support your decision.

1. In the 1960s, a group of black students walked around with signs that said "Down with segregation!"

2. A city police department would not allow women to join the police force.

3. A person accused of a serious crime refuses to give evidence against himself.

4. A town does not like the religious beliefs of a particular group, so it forbids that group to build a place where they can worship.

5. A woman accused of a serious crime wants a trial with a jury. The government says she doesn't have enough money for this type of trial.

6. A group of students who just turned eighteen want to vote for whom they would like as the next president of the United States.

7. The president of the United States wants to run for office again. This would be his/her third term.

Words like <u>let's</u> (let us), <u>you'll</u> (you will), etc., are contractions. Contractions that have the word <u>not</u> in them are called negatives. Other words like <u>nothing</u>, <u>never</u>, and <u>nobody</u> are also negatives. The rule is NEVER use double negatives when you write or speak. In these sentences, find the double negatives and rewrite the sentence in cursive, using the correct word.

EXAMPLE:
The fight didn't solve nothing. *The fight didn't solve anything.*

1. The team didn't want no trouble. _____

_____

2. Haven't you never seen Yellowstone Park? _____

_____

3. There weren't no eggs left in the carton. _____

_____

4. I haven't never been happier to finish a school year. _____

_____

5. This path doesn't lead nowhere. _____

_____

6. Can't no one in this class solve the puzzle? _____

_____

7. Richard didn't have nothing to read. _____

_____

8. Nanette said that she hadn't never thought of that idea. _____

_____

9. Don't spill none of the juice on the carpet. _____

_____

10. There isn't nothing you can do about the weather. _____

_____

Eggs? What eggs? Chicken eggs! Down through the ages, eggs have been eaten around the world. In America, the most popular eggs to eat are chicken eggs. Chicken eggs are classified primarily by their weight. Small eggs weigh approximately 18 ounces a dozen. Medium eggs weigh 21 ounces a dozen. Large eggs weigh 24 ounces a dozen. Extra large eggs weigh a hefty 27 ounces a dozen. Jumbo eggs, which are classified as the largest sellable eggs, weigh 30 ounces a dozen.

1. Six dozen _____ eggs weigh a total of 180 ounces.

2. How many eggs are in 6 dozen? _____

3. How many eggs are in 12 dozen? _____ What are two different ways you can use to find the answer to this question? _____, _____

4. Which weighs more—3 dozen jumbo eggs or 5 dozen small eggs?
_____

5. If 5 dozen eggs weigh a total of 150 ounces, which eggs would they be? _____

6. If you wanted to boil a total of 120 eggs for an Easter egg hunt and you wanted an equal number of each size of egg, how many of each size would you boil? _____

7. What is the minimum weight you can have if you have 4 dozen eggs? _____ ounces of _____ eggs.

8. If you bought a dozen of each size of egg, what should be the total weight in ounces? _____

9. Jan gathered 4 dozen medium-sized eggs, 3 dozen small eggs, 1 dozen large eggs, 2 dozen extra-large eggs, and $\frac{1}{2}$ dozen jumbo eggs. How many eggs did she gather? _____ How many ounces did she have altogether? _____

10. Mother bought 3 dozen eggs, but some broke on the way home. When she got home, she tried to divide them evenly between 2 bowls, but she had 1 left over. With 3 and 4 bowls she again had 1 left over. When she divided them into 5 bowls, they came out exactly even! How many eggs did she have? _____

Fill in the blanks with pronouns.

EXAMPLE: Maggie collects books. _____She_____ likes old books best.

1. Nancy's parents collect books also; _____ are professors.

2. Emily washed _____ hair.

3. I asked _____ sister to give _____ a ride home.

4. The cat washed _____ baby kittens.

5. The girls made lunch for _____ family.

6. "Craig, will _____ give _____ _____ phone number?"

The pronouns <u>we</u> and <u>us</u> are sometimes used with nouns. Fill in the blanks with <u>we</u> or <u>us</u>. Use <u>we</u> when the noun is the subject; use <u>us</u> when it is not.

7. _____ Americans have a lot of pride in our country.

8. At the dinner party, _____ guests made sandwiches.

9. The stranger made a map for _____ travelers.

10. Will the teacher give _____ students good grades?

Use just the letters from these spelling words to make three or four new words. Try to make four- and five-letter words. Use a letter only once in each word.

EXAMPLE:
journeys	_our_	_runs_	_yes_	_nose_
1. enemies				
2. intermediate				
3. vocabulary				
4. inscription				
5. purpose				
6. suspended				
7. examiner				
8. pendulum				
9. luxurious				
10. monotonous				

Choose a place you would like to go that you can drive to in a few days. Find a map and chart your course. Estimate, then check how many miles it is from your house. Decide how fast you can drive and how many hours you are going to travel each day. Using division, figure out how many days it will take. Make a chart using the information you have. Decide how long you can stay. Remember, you have to save some time to drive home. Try a one-week trip, then a three-week trip. Remember, you have to travel by car. Could you chart your results? Can you estimate the cost of your trip? Involve your parents in this plan to help you!

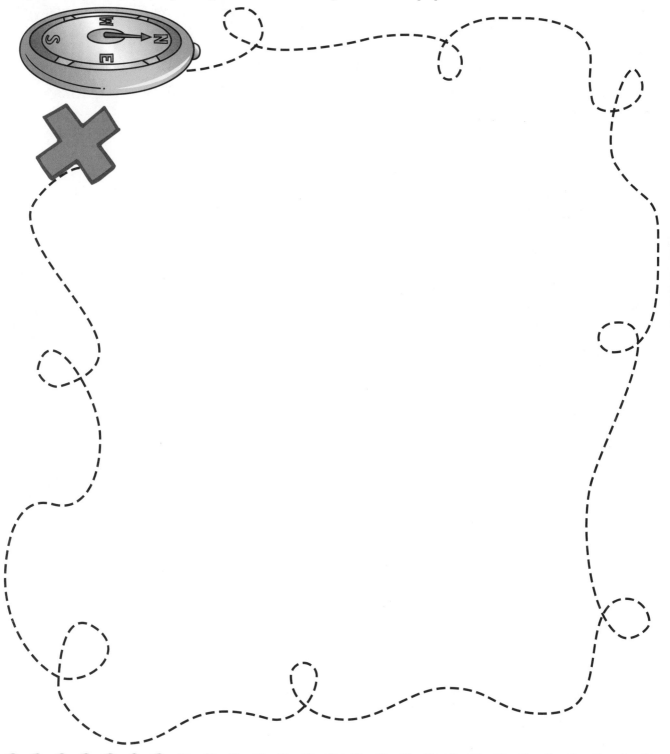

69

**More Pronouns. Use <u>I</u> or <u>me</u> in these sentences.
When <u>I</u> is part of a compound subject, use it last.**

EXAMPLE:

She and ___I___ made a cake.

1. Mom and ____ went to the store.

2. Will you come to see Ken and ____?

3. Karen asked ____ to answer the door.

4. Ann Marie and ____ ate our lunch out-side.

5. Snakes scare ____ to death.

6. The gift was sent by Aunt Jean and ___.

Use possessive pronouns in these sentences to show ownership.

7. Did you see _____ faces when they saw Santa?

8. _____ handwriting is very neat.

9. The prize is _____ for the asking.

10. _____ uncle, Clint, is coming for a visit.

11. The book you gave to Leza was _____.

12. The prints on the mirror are _____.

**Volcanoes. Answer <u>T</u> for true or <u>F</u> for false for the following statements.
If false, correct the sentence so it will be true.**

____ 1. A volcano is an opening in the crust of the earth through which lava, gases, ash, and rocks erupt.

____ 2. In a short time, volcanic material can build up to form mountains.

____ 3. These mountains can form only on land.

____ 4. All magma comes from the earth's core.

____ 5. Most volcanoes happen underwater.

____ 6. Mid-ocean ridges are formed from underwater volcanoes.

____ 7. Mid-ocean ridges happen when lava builds up under water and creates underwater mountain chains.

____ 8. Most volcanoes on land occur at diverging plate boundaries.

____ 9. Volcanoes on land occur on the edge of a continent or on islands.

____ 10. When two plates converge, compression forces rocks upward to make mountains.

Sharpen your skills with this timed multiplication test! Estimate how much time you think it will take you to do these problems. _____ Now do the actual test. How long did it take you to do it? _____ What's the difference between the two times? _____

1. 6 × 7 = _____
2. 12 × 2 = _____
3. 5 × 10 = _____
4. 9 × 6 = _____
5. 7 × 8 = _____
6. 11 × 12 = _____
7. 7 × 5 = _____
8. 11 × 2 = _____
9. 10 × 3 = _____
10. 5 × 6 = _____
11. 9 × 5 = _____
12. 8 × 4 = _____
13. 8 × 0 = _____
14. 6 × 12 = _____
15. 8 × 3 = _____
16. 10 × 2 = _____
17. 6 × 6 = _____
18. 8 × 9 = _____
19. 7 × 2 = _____
20. 8 × 7 = _____
21. 11 × 7 = _____
22. 5 × 2 = _____
23. 10 × 6 = _____
24. 9 × 4 = _____
25. 6 × 3 = _____

26. 8 × 9 = _____
27. 6 × 9 = _____
28. 11 × 10 = _____
29. 10 × 9 = _____
30. 9 × 11 = _____
31. 7 × 3 = _____
32. 12 × 10 = _____
33. 9 × 9 = _____
34. 8 × 8 = _____
35. 7 × 7 = _____
36. 10 × 10 = _____
37. 11 × 3 = _____
38. 6 × 5 = _____
39. 5 × 3 = _____
40. 9 × 2 = _____
41. 12 × 5 = _____
42. 10 × 0 = _____
43. 9 × 10 = _____
44. 8 × 2 = _____
45. 11 × 5 = _____
46. 8 × 8 = _____
47. 7 × 6 = _____
48. 7 × 7 = _____
49. 11 × 9 = _____
50. 5 × 12 = _____

51. 5 × 5 = _____
52. 9 × 0 = _____
53. 9 × 3 = _____
54. 7 × 4 = _____
55. 12 × 4 = _____
56. 9 × 9 = _____
57. 7 × 9 = _____
58. 8 × 5 = _____
59. 10 × 4 = _____
60. 9 × 8 = _____
61. 7 × 6 = _____
62. 10 × 5 = _____
63. 11 × 4 = _____
64. 7 × 8 = _____
65. 12 × 12 = _____
66. 9 × 7 = _____
67. 7 × 11 = _____
68. 5 × 4 = _____
69. 9 × 7 = _____
70. 10 × 8 = _____
71. 9 × 11 = _____
72. 8 × 12 = _____
73. 8 × 6 = _____
74. 12 × 3 = _____
75. 5 × 7 = _____

76. 11 × 5 = _____
77. 9 × 6 = _____
78. 9 × 12 = _____
79. 6 × 8 = _____
80. 7 × 10 = _____
81. 5 × 11 = _____
82. 10 × 10 = _____
83. 6 × 11 = _____
84. 12 × 11 = _____
85. 12 × 9 = _____
86. 8 × 7 = _____
87. 5 × 8 = _____
88. 0 × 8 = _____
89. 8 × 6 = _____
90. 11 × 8 = _____
91. 11 × 12 = _____
92. 10 × 7 = _____
93. 8 × 11 = _____
94. 11 × 6 = _____
95. 6 × 10 = _____
96. 6 × 4 = _____
97. 11 × 8 = _____
98. 12 × 6 = _____
99. 8 × 10 = _____
100. 12 × 12 = _____

Cover up the answers with another sheet of paper and try it again!

If the pronoun is not part of the subject it is an object pronoun.
Write SP if the pronoun is a subject pronoun.
Write OP if it is an object pronoun.

_____ 1. The funny story made <u>us</u> laugh.

_____ 2. McCall held the dance trophy in front of <u>her</u> and Ted.

_____ 3. Will <u>we</u> see any sharks at Sea Life Park?

_____ 4. Denise and <u>I</u> went ice skating with <u>her</u> family.

_____ 5. Don't give <u>her</u> the present until noon.

_____ 6. Did <u>they</u> fly or take the train home?

_____ 7. <u>We</u> are going to Washington, D.C., this summer.

_____ 8. Are <u>you</u> a cousin to Hal Tomyn?

_____ 9. <u>I</u> bought blue gym shoes this year because I like <u>them</u>.

_____ 10. The dog got <u>its</u> paw caught in the bear trap.

Regular verbs show action that happened in the past by adding -ed to the base word. But to show past tense for irregular verbs, you have to change the spelling.

EXAMPLE: sit - sat

In the square there are some irregular verbs. Write them under the correct heading below.

<u>Remember:</u> The past participle is used with a helping word when in a sentence.

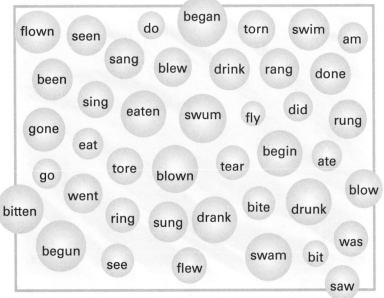

Present	Past	Past Participle

Clayton's mother bought him some new clothes for camp. She bought him 4 pairs of shorts—red, blue, green, and white. She also bought him 8 T-shirts—2 red, 2 blue, 2 green, and 2 white. She bought him 4 long-sleeved sweatshirts—2 white and 2 blue.

Use a tree diagram to organize the data to find out how many different choices of shorts and shirts Clayton can wear. _____ total choices

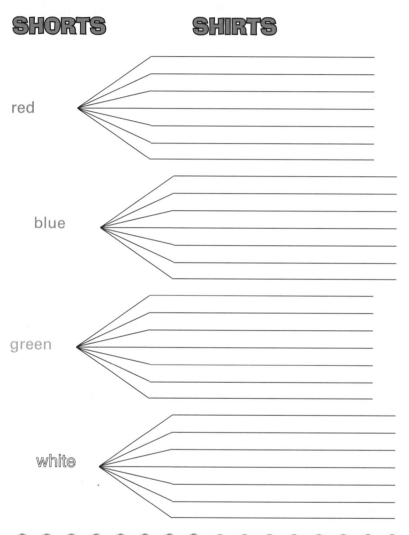

SHORTS　　**SHIRTS**

red

blue

green

white

Our government is divided into three branches. Each branch is given different, but equal, powers. In the circle below, write down the branch and the power it has; then draw a picture that could represent each branch.

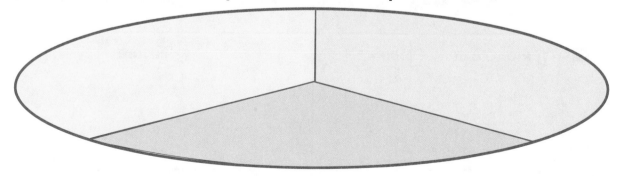

Below are some parts of sentences that give the cause. Finish the sentence by writing what the effect might be. Look for clue words.

EXAMPLE: (cause) The old house had not been painted for years,
(effect) so the first thing we did was paint it. (The clue word is "so.")

1. Our Thanksgiving turkey was burned because _____ .

2. _____ because my new shoes were too tight.

3. The wind was blowing hard, so _____ .

4. Because I didn't get up early enough this morning, _____ .

5. Some children were playing with matches; as a result, _____ .

Now it's your turn to write the cause to the effects.

6. The plane was delayed due to _____ .

7. _____ , my stomach hurt.

8. _____ , so we decided to celebrate.

9. The drinks were very sweet because _____ .

10. _____ , there was no fruit on the trees this summer.

In the table below, make a list of all the things you enjoy that use electricity. Now ask a parent, adult, or grandparent to list all the things that use electricity that they did not have when they were your age.

**Compare the differences and similarities on your table.
Next, create a list of things children in 30 years may have that use electricity that we do not have today. Be creative!**

You	Parent/Adult
Grandparent/Elderly Person	**Future**

Keep track of how much television you watch daily in a two-week period; then graph the results. Do the same with how much time you play computer games or TV games; then graph the results. Now do the same with how much time you spend with your friends; then graph the results. You can use the same graph for all three if you use different colored pens or pencils.

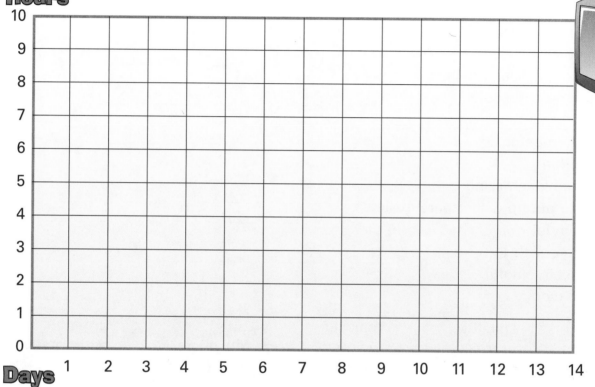

Hours

10
9
8
7
6
5
4
3
2
1
0

Days   1   2   3   4   5   6   7   8   9   10   11   12   13   14

Powers of the Government. Decide which branch of government (legislative, executive, or judicial) each statement describes.

_____ 1. can impeach the president of the United States

_____ 2. approves treaties

_____ 3. approves or vetoes bills

_____ 4. Interprets and examines laws and treaties

_____ 5. appoints justices

Adjectives modify or describe nouns and pronouns. Read the clues to help you do the crossword puzzle. The answers are adjectives that are listed in the word box below.

Across

1. satisfied
4. dignified, lofty, noble
8. filled with fear
11. critical, immediate
12. rough voice
13. courageous, valiant, gallant
14. headstrong, inflexible

Down

1. skilled, competent
2. commanding
3. unbelievable, amazing
5. unable to put up with others' beliefs
6. lively, playful
7. childish, foolish
9. ill-disposed, hateful
10. made of wood

hoarse	spiteful	majestic	silly	urgent
contented	horrified	wooden	obstinate	authoritative
stouthearted	fantastic	intolerant	frisky	capable

Quotation marks go before and after exactly what a person is saying and the titles of stories and songs. Tell why they are used in these sentences.

1. Robert asked, "What are the rules for this game?"
   _____

2. Mother was fixing lunch when David came home. "Please set the table," she said.
   _____

3. "What's that terrible noise?" cried Carla.
   _____

4. Cindy was playing "Tennessee Waltz" on her guitar when Pete came in.
   _____

Your turn. Put quotation marks in these sentences.

5. I don't think I can do this by myself, Marge sighed.
6. Hillary is singing America the Beautiful to her sister.
7. Do you like baseball or football best? Debra asked. I like baseball best.
8. Not me, answered Eleanor. I like basketball best.

Trickster

This plane demonstrates the movement of an airplane in response to the air it is traveling through. If you take time to work on your design, you can get your plane to soar like an eagle!

Stuff You Need:

paper (8 ½" × 11")
scissors

Here's What to Do:

1. Fold the upper edge of the paper over to the opposite side of the paper. (A) Unfold and repeat the same thing for the other side. You now have an X on your page. Now fold the top to the bottom of the X created by the first two folds. (B)

2. This is the tricky part. Fold the middle crease in on both sides, bringing the top corners toward the bottom of the X. Now the paper looks like a house. Use the illustrations to help you. (C)

3. Fold the tip of the roof to the gutter. (D)

4. Fold the airplane in half so that the folds are not showing. (E)

5. Fold the wings down. The body of the airplane should be no more than a half-inch tall. (F)

6. Fold the outer quarter-inch of the airplane wing up into the air. Tape the two wings together at the middle fold. (G)

7. Cut two small flaps out of the back of the wings in the sections illustrated. These will help direct the movement of the plane. (G)

8. By bending the flaps on the back of the wing, you can get the plane to bank either left or right. If you bend both flaps the same way, you can get the plane to climb sharply into the atmosphere or crash right into the dirt.

A.

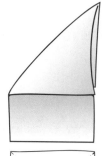

B.

C.

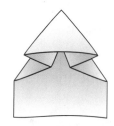

D.

E.

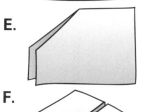

F.

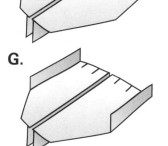

G.

You've Got a Lot of Nerve!

You are able to feel because of nerves. Some places have more nerves than others. Read ahead to see where people are most likely to "get on your nerves!"

Stuff You Need:

helper
paper clip

Here's What to Do:

1. Open up the paper clip so that the two endpoints are pointing in the same direction, at least 1 inch apart.

2. Ask a partner to place an arm on a table, palm facing up, and close his eyes. You are going to touch the paper clip to different parts of his fingers and arm and see if he can tell whether you are using one end of the paper clip or two.

3. Begin at the fingertips and touch two ends. Ask him if he feels one or two. Tell him if he is correct or incorrect. Do several fingers, changing from one to two points and back again.

4. Slowly move up, testing mid-fingers, palms, wrists, arms (both sides), and back. Change from one to two ends at random.

What's This All About?

Nerves, which detect when a body part is touched, are distributed all over the human body. However, nerves are not distributed evenly. Some parts of the body have many more nerves than others. By finding out where your friend can feel both ends of the paper clip, you also find out where the body's nerves are closest together. What do you notice about the function of the body parts that seem to have lots of nerves?

Summer Bridge Activities™

Motivational Calendar

Month _____

My parents and I decided that if I complete
15 days of **Summer Bridge Activities**™ and
read _____ minutes a day, my incentive/reward will be:

_____

Child's Signature _____ Parent's Signature_____

Day 1 ☆ 📖 ____	Day 9 ☆ 📖 ____
Day 2 ☆ 📖 ____	Day 10 ☆ 📖 ____
Day 3 ☆ 📖 ____	Day 11 ☆ 📖 ____
Day 4 ☆ 📖 ____	Day 12 ☆ 📖 ____
Day 5 ☆ 📖 ____	Day 13 ☆ 📖 ____
Day 6 ☆ 📖 ____	Day 14 ☆ 📖 ____
Day 7 ☆ 📖 ____	Day 15 ☆ 📖 ____
Day 8 ☆ 📖 ____	

Child: Color the ☆ for daily activities completed.
Color the 📖 for daily reading completed.

Parent: Initial the ____ when all activities are complete.

Discover Something New!

Fun Activity Ideas to Go Along with the Third Section!

 1. Draw a picture of your favorite friend, toy, or teacher in your favorite time of the year.

 2. Put together a collection of leaves from your neighborhood and label as many as you can.

 3. Write five questions that you would like to ask the president of the United States.

 4. Invent a new ice cream flavor. How is it made? What will you call it?

 5. Play football with a Frisbee.

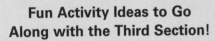 6. Find out how to recycle in your town; then make and deliver flyers to inform all your neighbors.

7. Using a book on astronomy, look for stars and constellations. This is a fun nighttime activity.

 8. Write your answer to the following question: How would the world be different without Alexander Graham Bell?

 9. Surprise your parents and weed a flower bed or garden, rake the leaves, do the dishes, etc.

 10. Pretend you live in the year 2028. How will life be different? How will you look? What will you eat? How will you get around? Write it down and draw it.

 11. Play flashlight tag, tonight!

 12. Design a comic strip and draw it.

 13. Paint a mural on butcher paper.

 14. Set up a miniature golf course in your own backyard.

 15. Play hockey using a broom.

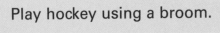

Division Outcomes. Complete this table to see which of these numbers can be divided by 2, 3, 5, 9, and 10 without having remainders. After you have finished the chart, see if you can come up with some hypotheses to form some divisibility rules.

Hypotheses of 2, 3, 5, 9, and 10

y = yes and n = no

2 Hypothesis
_____
_____
_____
_____

3 Hypothesis
_____
_____
_____
_____

5 Hypothesis
_____
_____
_____
_____

9 Hypothesis
_____
_____
_____
_____

10 Hypothesis
_____
_____
_____
_____

Divisible by	2	3	5	9	10
3,825	n	y	y	y	n
930					
792					
856					
1,440					
6,825					
41,004					
85,010					
314,402					
10,009,407					
9,617,590					

Try out your hypotheses on number combinations of your own to see if they really work.

Put an **X** by the words you might look up in a thesaurus to find synonyms for these words.

1. **leopard**
_____ animal
_____ fish
_____ insect
_____ horse

2. **story**
_____ complaint
_____ length
_____ plant
_____ drama

3. **fanfare**
_____ explanation
_____ metal
_____ religion
_____ music

Thesaurus

4. **sapling**
_____ plant
_____ spring
_____ vitamin
_____ tree

5. **cabin**
_____ payment
_____ habitation
_____ disease
_____ arms

6. **gold**
_____ metal
_____ fighting
_____ wisdom
_____ smoothness

Fill in the blank in each sentence with a synonym of the word in the box. Look in the dictionary if you need help.

EXAMPLE:

I had to |finish| *complete* my work before I could go with my friends.

1. Sarah and Angie go for a |walk| _____ every day except Sunday.

2. It's fun to watch the little colts |play| _____ in the green pastures.

3. The electricians have done |enough| _____ work for this week.

4. I cannot |find| _____ the information I |need| _____ for my report.

5. You will have to |write| _____ all the important events of your |trip| _____.

6. The lost couple had not had any |food| _____ for six days.

7. Will you please |show| _____ how your new invention works?

8. They will |try| _____ to climb Mount Everest again next summer.

9. Tourists |might| _____ be able to travel to the moon by the year 2010.

10. The value of this coin will |grow| _____ over the years.

Read each passage on electricity. One sentence in each passage is false. Cross out the false sentence and try to correct it. Then answer the question after each passage.

1. An electrical current is moving energy. You can see electricity at work in lights, motors, computers, and some toys. Any material that allows an electric current to pass through is called a battery.

   Question: How many things can you think of in 1–2 minutes that need electricity? Have a race with someone to see who can think of the most ideas.

2. Material that does not allow an electric current to pass through it is called a circuit. This material covers conducting materials. It stops electricity from escaping and causing harm.

   Question: What are 5 things you can do to ensure safe use of electricity in your home?

   1. _____ 2. _____ 3. _____

   4. _____ 5. _____

Round the Clock Multiplication. Choose numbers between 10 and 100 and put them in the outer circle. Next, put numbers between 1 and 12 in the following circle. Then multiply the outer circle's number by the second circle's number.

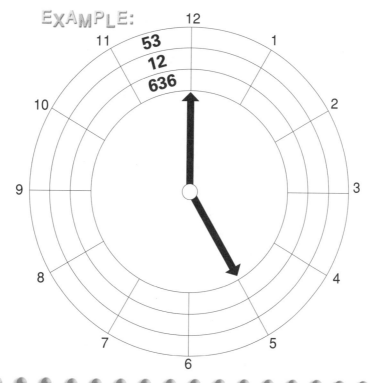

EXAMPLE:

53
12
636

Hunters, trappers, and pioneers moved west in the 1800s. Take 5 minutes to brainstorm all the things you would need for a trip west. List as many things as you can! Now take this list and think of different categories in which these items would fit. For example, one category might be food.

What double consonants go in these spelling words?

1. i ____ ____ ediately

2. su ____ ____ osed

3. su ____ ____ ort

4. po ____ ____ ible

5. i ____ ____ egular

6. inte ____ ____ igence

7. a ____ ____ ribute

8. a ____ ____ egiance

9. di ____ ____ erence

10. bu ____ ____ ernut

11. a __ __e__ __ ment

12. i ____ ____ ocent

13. i ____ ____ emovable

14. di ____ ____ atisfied

15. a ____ ____ reviation

16. a ____ ____ e ____ ____ ible

17. exce ____ ____ ence

18. scri ____ ____ le

19. a ____ ____ ual

20. permi ____ ____ ing

● ●

Health—Eyes. Label the parts of the eye below using the following words:

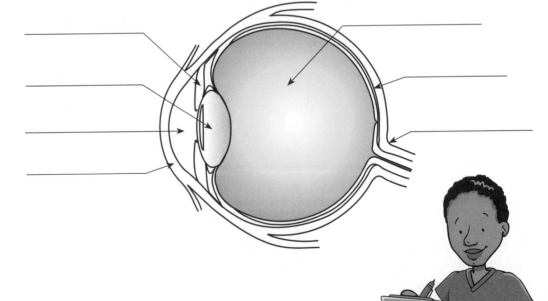

retina

cornea

lens

iris

pupil

vitreous humor

optic nerve

Make a journal of all the activities you do in one day. Look back over the activities at the end of the day. Imagine that you could not see. How would this have affected your day? What would you have needed to do differently?

● ●

Polyominoes.

1. These are all polyominoes.

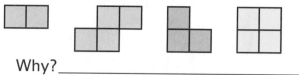

    Why?_____

2. These are not polyominoes.

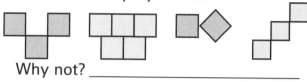

    Why not? _____

3. Draw some polyominoes of your own using 5 squares.

4. Chart the course by following lines according to the instructions above the graph. How many polyominoes did you chart? _____

east 1, north 3, east 5, north 3, east 1, south 5, east 1, north 3, west 5, south 4, west 2, north 6, west 1, north 3, east 2, south 2, east 5, north 1, west 3, north 1, east 4, south 1, east 1, south 6, west 1, south 2, west 8, and you should be back where you started from.

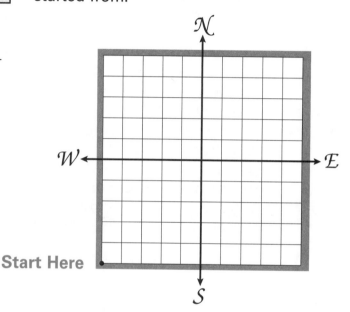

Start Here

Put into sequence the following steps on how a bill can become a law. Then come up with a bill you think should become a law. Draw a comic strip that shows characters putting these steps into action.

____ Get the president to approve.

____ Write a bill.

____ Get a majority vote in Congress.

____ If the president vetoes the bill, then it may become a law by $\frac{2}{3}$ vote in Congress.

Your own bill: _____

"The Eagle Has Landed."

American astronauts Neil Armstrong and Buzz Aldrin became the first men on the moon on July 20, 1969. The giant Apollo moon rocket was 363 feet high and weighed six and a half million pounds.

The Lunar Module (LM) left the Apollo at 1:45 P.M. "The Eagle has wings," Armstrong stated. At 3:46 the LM emerged from behind the moon. "The burn was on time," reported Armstrong matter-of-factly. At that time, they were at an altitude of about 20 miles, descending toward 50,000 feet. The astronauts had to make the all-important and final decision whether to remain in orbit or to descend to the lunar surface to make the landing.

At approximately 4:07 P.M., Armstrong pressed the button marked "Proceed." Aldrin and Armstrong realized in horror that the computer-controlled guidance system was taking them right down into a football-field-sized crater with a large number of big boulders and rocks. With only precious seconds to spare, Armstrong took manual control of the spacecraft. He searched for and found a clear area amid the menacing rock field below. "Houston," Armstrong radioed, "Tranquility base here. The Eagle has landed."

It was the first time men from earth had touched down on the moon. Armstrong was the first human being to set foot on the lunar surface. As his left foot touched the moon to take the first step, he spoke the now famous words, "That's one small step for man, one giant leap for mankind."

1. What was Armstrong referring to when he said "The Eagle has landed"?

2. The word lunar is used several times. What is another word for lunar?

3. What did "all-important and final decision" really mean to the astronauts?

4. What was the real significance of this mission to humankind?

5. What does this report tell you about what type of men Armstrong and Aldrin are?

Two electrical pathways are series circuits and two are parallel circuits. Label the pictures as either a series circuit or parallel circuit.

_____   _____   _____   _____

Find the missing numbers and then write the rule.

1.	M	N		2.	M	N		3.	M	N		4.	M	N
	15	20			25	36			54	45			9	72
	40	45			19	30			89	80			11	88
	90	__			57	__			73	__			7	__
	35	__			__	84			__	61			5	__

Rule: **M + 5 = N** Rule: **M + 11 = N** Rule: **M –** Rule: **M ×**

5.	M	N		6.	M	N		7.	M	N		8.	M	N
	8	48			21	7			48	8			36	24
	4	24			30	10			12	2			57	45
	10	__			18	__			__	7			63	__
	6	__			12	__			24	__			__	78

Rule: _____ Rule: _____ Rule: _____ Rule: _____

9.	M	N		10.	M	N		11.	M	N		12.	M	N
	7	63			10	120			3.2	5.5			35	50
	__	81			__	144			7.1	__			73	__
	__	54			9	108			__	7.3			__	42
	3	27			__	132			4.4	__			100	__

Rule: _____ Rule: _____ Rule: _____ Rule: _____

Do research on the Trail of Tears. Write a poem about this event using the letters of Trail of Tears at the beginning of each line. Be sure to include the emotions felt at this time. Make a border around the poem with colors and objects you feel would best describe the mood of your poem.

T _____

R _____

A _____

I _____

L _____

O _____

F _____

T _____

E _____

A _____

R _____

S _____

Contents and Index. Read this fictitious contents and index from a history book. Then answer the questions below.

Contents

1. The Nation Grows 216
   Exploring the West 217
   Louisiana Purchase. 222
   War of 1812 229
   Country Growth 236

2. The Civil War 250
   The Beginning 251
   The Two Sides 260
   The First Part of War 270
   The Second Part 289
   The Civil War at Sea 300

Maps R60

Glossary R95

Index

Civil War 250–300
   background 254–255
   problems after 304–310
Economy 97, 319, 420
   after American Revolution . 97–100
   after Civil War 319
   of Great Lakes 400
Jackson, Andrew . . . 100–101, 124–130
Louisiana Purchase 222
Massasoit 172
Native Americans
   see American Indians
Water 5-6, 12, 21–25, 610

1. What is the difference between the contents and the index in books?
   _____

2. If you wanted to know if this book had a section on the War of 1812, where would you look?_____

3. If you wanted to see if there was a picture of Andrew Jackson in the book, where would you look?_____

4. Where would you look to find out who fought in the Civil War?_____

5. How many sections are in chapter one? _____

6. On what page would you look to find out about Native Americans? ___

7. On what page could you look to learn who Massasoit was? _____

8. How many sections are there about the Civil War? _____

9. What information is in the glossary of books?_____

A <u>simile</u> is a figure of speech in which two unlike things are compared using <u>like</u> or <u>as</u>. Write the actual meaning of these similes.

1. Her voice lilted like soft music.
   _____

2. It was like a movie, except it was not on a screen.
   _____

Match the term to the math definition dealing with fractions.

1. fraction
2. improper fraction
3. quotient
4. mixed number
5. denominator
6. numerator

a. The answer you get by dividing one number by another number

b. The number found below the line in a fraction

c. A number that names a part of a set or part of a whole

d. The number found above the line in a fraction

e. A number that has a whole number and a fraction

f. A fraction whose numerator is greater than its denominator or can be equal to its denominator

Show your understanding.

7. Show $2 \div 9$ as a fraction. _____

8. $82 \div 7$ can be written $\frac{82}{7}$ or $7\overline{)82}$.

What is the divisor? _____

What is the remainder? _____

Write it as a mixed number. _____

9. Show $15 \div 7$ as an improper fraction. _____

10. What kind of fractions are these: $\frac{28}{5}$ $\frac{17}{12}$ $\frac{59}{7}$? _____

Write a mixed number for each.

_____ _____ _____

Remember...

- The <u>range</u> is the difference between the highest number and the lowest number in the data.
- To calculate the <u>mean</u> (or average), add the list of numbers and then divide by the number of items.
- The <u>median</u> is the middle number that appears in the data.
- The <u>mode</u> is the number that appears most often in the data.

Use the chart to answer the questions about the number of medals awarded at the 2000 Summer Olympic Games held in Sydney, Australia.

1. What is the range of the data?

2. What is the mode of the data?

3. What is the median of the data?

4. What is the average number of medals awarded?

Country	Number of Medals
United States	97
Russia	88
China	59
Australia	58
Germany	57
France	38
Italy	34
Cuba	29
Britain	28
South Korea	28
Romania	26

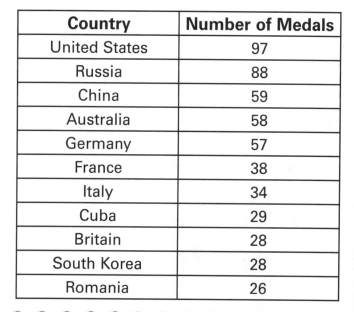

People, young and old, often jump to conclusions. They frequently make up their minds without looking for facts or reasons behind a situation. Write a conclusion for each situation given and then think of facts you need to verify your conclusion.

1. There is a large package with your name on it at your doorstep without a note saying who it's from. It's not your birthday.

   Conclusion:

   Facts needed:

2. Your teacher sends a note home with you addressed directly to your parents. He/she tells you to make sure your parents get it.

   Conclusion:

   Facts needed:

3. When you go to the game, no one will speak to you or play with you.

   Conclusion:

   Facts needed:

4. The house is dark and the doors are locked when you get home.

   Conclusion:

   Facts needed:

5. You have looked all through the house and all over the yard, and you cannot find your pet turtle.

   Conclusion:

   Facts needed:

Natural Resources. Create a poster that reminds us of the importance of the 3 Rs: Reduce, Reuse, and Recycle!

Add to find the fraction. The sum is found in the center.

$\dfrac{1}{8}$

EXAMPLE:

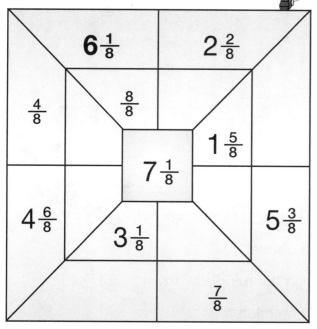

$6\frac{1}{8}$ $2\frac{2}{8}$

$\frac{4}{8}$ $\frac{8}{8}$

$1\frac{5}{8}$

$7\frac{1}{8}$

$4\frac{6}{8}$ $3\frac{1}{8}$ $5\frac{3}{8}$

$\frac{7}{8}$

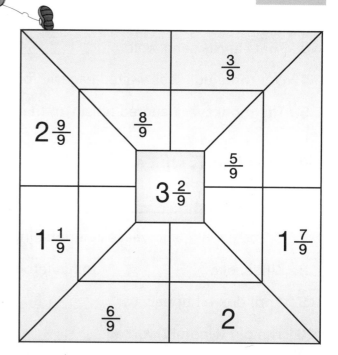

$\frac{3}{9}$

$2\frac{9}{9}$ $\frac{8}{9}$

$\frac{5}{9}$

$3\frac{2}{9}$

$1\frac{1}{9}$ $1\frac{7}{9}$

$\frac{6}{9}$ 2

Label the drawing and fill in the outline below with the terms in the proper sequential order; then explain how sound waves reach the brain through the ears.

cochlea   stirrup   pinna   auditory canal   hammer   anvil   eardrum

I. Outer Ear

   A.

II. Middle Ear

   A.

   B.

   C.

   D.

   E.

III. Inner Ear

   A.

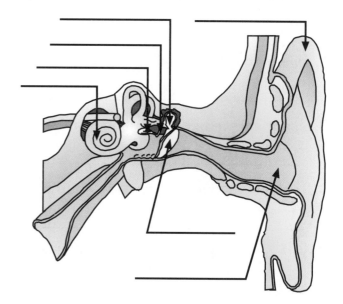

Underline the adverb in each sentence. At the end of the sentence, write the word it modifies.

1. The cat's broken leg hurts badly. _____

2. The train moved rapidly down the tracks. _____

3. That chorus sang well. _____

4. Our three bulldogs waited eagerly for their walk. _____

5. The monkeys chattered noisily in the trees. _____

Fill in the blanks with adverbs.

6. The child sat _____ on the stairs.

7. Delicate white snowflakes were falling _____ to the ground.

8. Kirk spoke _____ to his father on the phone.

9. April drove her new car _____ through the middle of town.

10. The old windmill worked _____ after he oiled it.

Categories. Find the word that does not belong in the category. Draw a line through it and write a sentence using the word you drew a line through to tell why it doesn't belong.

EXAMPLE:

street - road - ~~railroad~~ - freeway - highway *Cars do not travel on a railroad.*

1. software - mouse - depth - program - disk _____

_____

2. dawn - daytime - twilight - sunrise - hyphen _____

_____

3. spaghetti - meatballs - menu - rhubarb - lasagna _____

_____

4. cyclone - generator - tornado - hurricane - monsoon_____

_____

5. mythology - petrology - geology - biology - zoology _____

_____

Watching for Zeros with Decimals.
Remember the extra zeros when necessary.

1. 41.5
    × 0.17

2. 1.09
    × 0.68

3. 3.05
    × 85.2

4. 0.003
    × 3.9

5. 7.4
    × 0.07

6. 0.09
    × 2.3

7. 0.035
    × 0.02

8. 0.005
    × 55

9. 27.5
    × 0.91

10. 60
    × 0.005

11. 0.92
    × 12.5

12. 1.08
    × 2.03

• •

Read the following scenarios. After reading each sentence, determine whether proper first aid procedures were being followed. Make a smiley face if they were done correctly. Make an X if they were not done correctly.

Scenario 1: Dallin fell off his bike and saw a big bruise forming on his leg.
____ He immediately put ice on it.
____ Next, he used compression by applying pressure with a cloth on the bruise.
____ Dallin then elevated his leg.

Scenario 2: While Jana and Adam were playing, a dog bit Adam.
____ Jana chased the dog for two blocks trying to capture it.
____ When she came back, Jana called her mom to help Adam.
____ Jana thought they should put butter on the wound.
____ Jana's mom washed the bite with soap and water.
____ They took Adam to the doctor's office.
____ Jana's mom called animal control.

Scenario 3: Linda felt dizzy and fainted.
____ Stephen quickly caught her from falling.
____ He gently put her to the floor and raised her feet.
____ He turned Linda's face to the side in case she vomited.
____ Mac suggested they slap or throw water on Linda to wake her up.
____ Stephen said, "No, let's get an adult to help us."

*As a child, an important thing to remember with first aid is to get emergency help. Make a card of phone numbers you can call in case of an emergency. Put it by your phone.

Answer T for true or F for false to the following statements about a discussion group. Tell why you think the false statements are false.

____ 1. You talk with others about an idea.

____ 2. The leader of the group should do most of the talking.

____ 3. The leader's only job is to keep things moving.

____ 4. It is important to listen to what is being said.

____ 5. Everyone should have a turn to talk.

____ 6. The people in the group should not ask questions.

____ 7. Disagreeing is okay in a discussion group.

____ 8. One of the leader's duties is to keep order.

____ 9. All participants should be polite to one another.

____ 10. The discussion leader should sum up what has been decided or discussed at the end of the session.

Pollution is a problem that affects all people on the earth.
Match the definition with the correct word.
Put a smiley face in the column if this term helps with pollution problems.
Put a sad face if it does not help our environment. If it is a sad face, come up with an idea of how we can improve in this area!

	Smiley or Sad	Idea

1. a tanker runs aground and leaks oil

2. energy generated from falling water

3. food for gardens from leaves and clippings

4. exhaust from cars and pollution from factories create a layer of pollution; heat rays from sun cannot go back into the atmosphere

5. energy generated from the inside of the earth

6. poisonous materials like paint thinner

7. saving

8. smoke and exhaust that mix with water vapor

9. waste taken to a dump that is eventually covered with earth

____ greenhouse effect

____ hazardous waste

____ acid rain

____ compost

____ conservation

____ geothermal energy

____ hydroelectric energy

____ landfill

____ oil spill

Finding the Circumference.

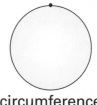

showing the
radius of a
circle

showing the
diameter of a
circle

circumference
is the distance
around a circle

Remember: To find the circumference of a circle, you must multiply the diameter by 3.14. With this information, complete the missing data in the table below.

	Radius of the Circle	Diameter of the Circle	Circumference of the Circle
1.	12 mm	24 mm	75.36 mm
2.	11 inches	22 inches	
3.		18 cm	
4.	10 meters		
5.	13 yards		
6.			150.72 feet
7.		42 inches	
8.	17 cm		
9.			282.60 mm
10.			314 inches

Women's Rights. Because of women such as Lucy Stone, Susan B. Anthony, Lucretia Mott, Elizabeth Cady Stanton, and Sarah and Angelina Grimke, women have many rights today that they didn't have in earlier times. Research one of these women and write of the trials she had to go through because of what she believed.

95

Adjectives tell how many, what kind, or which one about the nouns or pronouns they modify. Fill in the blanks with these kinds of adjectives. Use two adjectives telling how many, two telling what kind, and one telling which one. At the end of the sentence, tell which kind you used.

1. _____ cars got stuck in the traffic jam. _____

2. _____ adventure was the most exciting I've ever had. _____

3. The _____ teddy bear cost twenty-five dollars. _____

4. There were _____ camels than lions at the zoo. _____

5. The _____ lizard that came after us was huge. _____

Articles: Special Adjectives (a, an, the). Circle the correct word.

6. Was that (a, an, the) alligator or (a, an) crocodile we saw back there?

7. The student gave her teacher (a, an) crisp, red apple.

8. (A, An, The) excited child was playing with (a, an) fluffy kitten.

9. After (a, an) rainstorm (a, an, the) sun glistens on (a, an, the) puddles.

10. If March comes in like (a, an, the) lion, it should go out like (a, an, the) lamb.

Take a word from list A and a word from list B to make compound words. Write the compound word in the middle. A word in list B could be the first word in the compound.

A			B	
craft	ware	1. _____	speaker	wreck
loud	blood	2. _____	silver	writer
ship	guard	3. _____	wrist	board
vine	clip	4. _____	yard	pepper
anchor	mint	5. _____	neck	woman
watch	turtle	6. _____	space	bite
type	frost	7. _____	hound	life
print		8. _____	news	

1. _____
2. _____
3. _____
4. _____
5. _____
6. _____
7. _____
8. _____
9. _____
10. _____
11. _____
12. _____
13. _____
14. _____
15. _____

Multiplying Fractions Pictures.

Question: How do you picture what $\frac{1}{2}$ of $\frac{1}{2}$ is?

Picture [ ] $\frac{1}{2}$ of a box as $\frac{1}{2}$ of 1. Now picture what $\frac{1}{2}$ of $\frac{1}{2}$ is. [ ]

So $\frac{1}{2}$ of $\frac{1}{2} = \frac{1}{4}$, or $1 \div 2 \div 2 = \frac{1}{4}$.

With the above information, illustrate and answer the following multiplication problems. Reduce to the simplest terms.
<u>Remember</u>: When you multiply fractions, the product gets <u>smaller</u>.

1. $\frac{1}{2} \times \frac{3}{4} =$ _____

2. $\frac{1}{4} \times \frac{1}{2} =$ _____

3. $\frac{1}{2} \times \frac{1}{3} =$ _____

4. $\frac{1}{3} \times \frac{2}{3} =$ _____

5. $\frac{2}{3} \times \frac{1}{6} =$ _____

6. $\frac{1}{3} \times \frac{1}{4} =$ _____

7. $\frac{2}{3} \times \frac{4}{5} =$ _____

8. $\frac{2}{3} \times \frac{2}{3} =$ _____

9. $\frac{1}{4} \times \frac{2}{3} =$ _____

10. $\frac{3}{4} \times \frac{2}{5} =$ _____

Early Inventions in America. Match the inventor with his invention. Then sketch an invention of your own and explain in detail how it would work and why it would be a good idea.

_____ Eli Whitney   **a.** telegraph

_____ Elias Howe   **b.** phonograph

_____ Levi Strauss   **c.** sewing machine

_____ Cyrus McCormick   **d.** cotton gin

_____ Samuel F. B. Morse   **e.** telephone

_____ Thomas Edison   **f.** reaper

_____ Alexander G. Bell   **g.** blue jeans

More than one adjective can be used to modify the same noun. Underline the adjectives in the sentences. Circle the word they modify.

1. The wild, eerie wind frightened the animals.

2. A fuzzy, brown caterpillar was creeping down the sidewalk.

3. Staci splashed some fresh, cool water on her face.

4. The hot, tired explorers swam in a large, clear lake.

5. The spicy aroma of apple cider filled Jason's small, warm tent.

Some adjectives are used to compare. Add -er or -est to these adjectives to complete the sentences.

6. The (rainy) _____ spot in the world is in Hawaii.

7. Our back door is (wide) _____ than our front door.

8. Mozart was one of the world's (young) _____ composers.

9. I think the gorilla is one of the (ugly) _____ of all the apes.

10. New Jersey is one of the (small) _____ states.

Answer these questions Yes or No. Use the dictionary for help.

1. Is a gizzard a kind of bird? ____

2. Would the boy wear his mukluk? ____

3. Could you work as a gofer? ____

4. Do you wear a goatee on your head? ____

5. Could you play with a googol? ____

6. Would you sit on a cloy? ____

7. Is a truffle a rich chocolate candy? ____

8. Could you plant a vetch? ____

9. Can a little girl wear aarf? ____

10. Does yep mean yes? ____

11. Is a yeti mysterious? ____

12. Could animals be kept in a sedge? ____

13. Is an orlop part of a ship? ____

14. Can you live in a yurt? ____

15. Would you chop wood with an italic? ____

16. Would you eat a mango? ____

17. Can you drive an osier? ____

18. Is a flit a song or tune? ____

Practice Multiplying Fractions.
Remember to multiply the numerators, then multiply the denominators.

1. $\frac{1}{2} \times \frac{3}{4} =$ 2. $\frac{2}{3} \times \frac{2}{3} =$ 3. $\frac{3}{4} \times \frac{1}{4} =$ 4. $\frac{2}{3} \times \frac{5}{7} =$

5. $\frac{4}{5} \times \frac{2}{7} =$ 6. $\frac{1}{6} \times \frac{5}{6} =$ 7. $\frac{1}{3} \times \frac{2}{3} =$ 8. $\frac{3}{4} \times \frac{5}{6} =$

9. $\frac{5}{9} \times \frac{3}{4} =$ 10. $\frac{7}{8} \times \frac{2}{5} =$ 11. $\frac{3}{5} \times \frac{3}{10} =$ 12. $\frac{6}{7} \times \frac{3}{4} =$

Multiply. Write each product in its simplest form.

13. $\frac{1}{2} \times \frac{1}{6} \times \frac{2}{3} =$ —— or ——   14. $\frac{2}{3} \times \frac{5}{6} \times \frac{1}{4} =$ —— or ——

15. $\frac{1}{3} \times \frac{5}{7} \times \frac{3}{5} =$ —— or —— or ——   16. $\frac{2}{3} \times \frac{3}{4} \times \frac{1}{2} =$ —— or ——

17. $\frac{8}{9} \times \frac{1}{3} \times \frac{3}{4} =$ —— or ——   18. $\frac{2}{3} \times \frac{1}{2} \times \frac{3}{8} =$ —— or ——

Civil War. Look at the list below. Some of the terms have to do with the Civil War. Circle in gray the terms that refer to the Confederate side or a Confederate victory. Circle in blue the terms that refer to the Union side or a Union victory. Circle in red the terms that occurred in other periods of history.

Abraham Lincoln	Fort Duquesne	Valley Forge
Sally Tompkins	General Robert E. Lee	Frederick Douglass
Saratoga	General Ulysses S. Grant	Bill of Rights
Battle of Bull Run	Andrew Jackson	General Robert E. Lee
1776	Seven Days' Battle	Thomas Jefferson
Paul Revere	John Paul Jones	Jefferson Davis
Antietam	Eli Whitney	General William T. Sherman
Yorktown	Harriet Tubman	General Thomas "Stonewall" Jackson

Adverbs are words that modify or describe verbs, adjectives, and other adverbs. Adverbs tell how, when, and where. Many end with -ly. Use these adverbs to answer the questions in the chart.

immediately	far	there	nearly	inside
softly	lately	slowly	carefully	wildly
today	often	upstairs	eagerly	hard
closely	soon	never		

When ?						
How ?						
Where ?						

Write down the consequence of each act and how it could have been prevented by safety.

Act	Consequence	How It Could Have Been Prevented
1. Tripping on a toy		
2. Running in halls		
3. Swimming without a lifeguard		
4. Playing with matches		
5. Playing near broken glass		
6. Not wearing a seat belt		
7. Not wearing a helmet when biking		

Using a separate sheet of paper, draw a fire escape plan for your house. Make sure you have a meeting point outside for your family. Share your drawing with your family.

Angles. Fill in the blanks.

When two rays share the same endpoint they form an **(1.)** _____.

This endpoint is called the **(2.)** _____ of the angle. The

(3.) _____ is the unit used for measuring angles. A **(4.)** _____ is used to

measure angles. A **(5.)** _____ is marked with **(6.)** _____ degrees. You place

the center of the protractor on the vertex of the angle.

　　The **(7.)** _____ angle looks like a square corner. It measures **(8.)** _____

degrees. An **(9.)** _____ angle is smaller than a right angle, or less than 90 degrees.

An **(10.)** _____ angle is larger than a right angle, or greater than 90 degrees.

Label these three angles.

11. _____ 　　　　12. _____ 　　　　13. _____

Use your protractor to measure these angles.

14. _____ 　　15. _____ 　　16. _____ 　　17. _____

Use your protractor to draw an angle for these measures.

18. 75° 　　　　　　　19. 60° 　　　　　　　20. 15°

Proofread and circle the mistakes in the following paragraphs. Then rewrite the paragraphs, correcting the mistakes in spelling, punctuation, etc. Write in cursive. Try to find thirty-nine mistakes.

today the term "Native American" is used to descibe those people indigenous to america. however the firt explorers who came to America referred to them as "Indians" unknown to the exploders, most tribes had their own names. for example names used by the deleware indians of eastern north america meant "genuine men."

the Indians' languages way of life, and homes wer all very different. The aztic and maya Indians of central america built large citys The apache and Paiute used brush and mating to make simple huts the plains indians buit coneshaped tepees covered with buffalo skns Cliff dwellers and other Pueblo groups usd sun-dried bricks to make many-storyed houses

_____

_____

_____

_____

_____

_____

_____

_____

• •

Use homophones or homonyms to fill in these blanks. Remember: They are words that sound or are spelled the same, but mean different things.

EXAMPLE:

_____I_____ think _____I_____ have something in my _____eye_____.

1. Chris will _____ catching a bumble _____ for his insect collection.

2. My _____ Lola had an _____ bite her toe.

3. The _____ was _____ from playing at the concert.

4. _____ visit the _____ of Man in June.

5. Please _____ the door to the _____ closet.

6. Patt _____ me one _____ for good luck.

7. My _____ jeans _____ away in the wind.

8. We went _____ the mall to _____ some cards.

9. My brother _____ _____ pancakes for breakfast.

10. _____, I do not _____ how to play a musical instrument.

• •

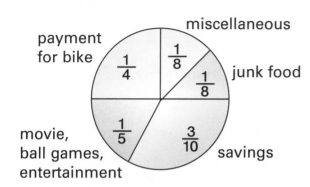

Circle graphs compare parts of a whole.

Day 12

Jake earns $20 a week doing chores for his neighbors. This circle graph shows how he uses his money.

1. How much money does Jake spend on junk food each week? $_____

2. How much on entertainment? $_____

3. How much on debts? $_____

4. How much does he save? $_____

5. Miscellaneous $_____

Bar graphs help you to compare data at a glance.

Valley Fair Music Place recorded the different types of music it sold during the summer months.

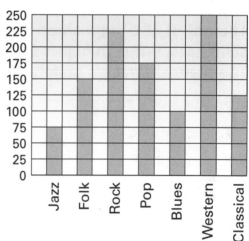

6. Which was the most popular? _____

7. Which sold the least? _____

8. What is the difference between the greatest and the least sold? _____

9. Which type of music came out with the average number sold? _____

10. Which is your favorite kind? _____

A pictograph uses picture symbols to represent data or specific units.

Riverton School kept track of how many parents visited their school during Parent Week. They made a pictograph to show the students the results.

Each 🚶 = 10 parents

11. Which day did most parents come? _____

12. What does 🚶 represent? _____

13. How many parents visited the school during Parent Week? _____

14. What other type of graph could you have used to show this data? _____

Prepositions are words that show certain relationships between other words. The words below are prepositions.

before	between	after	during	until	to
of	with	behind	near	above	through
for	under	off	across	from	in

Cross out the underlined words, and use one of the prepositions above to show a different relationship between these words.

EXAMPLE:

1. Grayson found his backpack ~~Under~~ _near_ his desk.

2. Julie stood ~~beside~~ _____ me at the parade.

3. Did you leave this box ~~on~~ _____ the bench?

4. The children will play ~~after~~ _____ dark.

5. The bats flew ~~into~~ _____ the window.

The object of a preposition is the noun or pronoun following it. In these sentences, write an object (noun or pronoun) for each preposition. The prepositions are underlined.

6. That boy had a glass <u>of</u> _____.

7. We climbed <u>over</u> a _____.

8. Amy fell <u>off</u> her _____.

9. Far <u>below</u> the _____ we could see the river.

10. Denise and Natalie are <u>from</u> _____.

Cross out the misspelled word and write it correctly above the list.

1. _____
   bicycle
   motorcicle
   unicycle
   cycler

2. _____
   symphony
   synonym
   antonym
   encyclopidiu

3. _____
   opposite
   oportunity
   opposed
   appearance

4. _____
   exhaost
   exhibit
   exist
   exceed

5. _____
   gypsy
   pearamid
   paralyze
   syllable

6. _____
   doughnut
   straght
   design
   twilight

7. _____
   unfamilar
   unsatisfactory
   unusual
   united

8. _____
   cruelty
   luxury
   enjoyable
   carfree

Day 13

Percentage is the comparison of a number to 100.

EXAMPLE: $\frac{15}{100} = 15\%$ 15 to 100 = 15%   15:100 = 15%

Write each ratio as a percent.

1. $\frac{20}{100}$ = ____	2. $\frac{50}{100}$ = ____	3. $\frac{3}{100}$ = ____	4. $\frac{47}{100}$ = ____
5. 9 to 100 = ____	6. 33 to 100 = ____	7. 14 to 100 = ____	8. 1 to 100 = ____
9. 75:100 = ____	10. 69:100 = ____	11. 81:100 = ____	12. 7:100 = ____

Write each percent in the form of a fraction.

13. 19% =	14. 87% =	15. 99% =	16. 24% =
17. 36% =	18. 55% =	19. 8% =	20. 63% =

Write each percentage in the lowest terms of a fraction.

21. 50% = $\frac{50}{100}$ = $\frac{1}{2}$ 22. 20% = ____ = ____   23. 70% = ____ = ____

24. 90% = ____ = ____   25. 45% = ____ = ____   26. 25% = ____ = ____

27. 4% = ____ = ____   28. 2% = ____ = ____   29. 80% = ____ = ____

Progress in the 1800s. Many changes occurred in America with the coming of the railroad, mining, and farming. These events encouraged more and more people to move west. Read and answer the following questions.

1. "Progress cannot be stopped." Do you agree with this statement? Why or why not?

2. Should we stop progress if it is hurting others or their rights are being ignored? Why or why not?

3. How does progress relate to the American Indians being placed on reservations in the 1800s?

4. List some modern examples of progress that hinder the rights of others. Are you in favor of these examples of progress? Why or why not?

The preposition and its object are called a prepositional phrase. Below are some phrases. Underline those that are prepositional phrases. Think about what words are prepositions. Refer to page 104 for help.

EXAMPLE: <u>past</u> <u>him</u>

1. between first and second base
2. near the broken bottle
3. a light hung
4. on your own paper
5. the messy streets
6. animals having four
7. along the trail
8. the circus elephant
9. outside the back door
10. under the house
11. your guide
12. until four o'clock
13. the science experiment
14. are the bridges
15. in the barn
16. how you will be
17. through the bushes

Health Problems and Pollution.
Complete each statement with the correct word listed below.

noise pollution
Environmental Protection Agency (EPA)

pollution
carbon monoxide

radon
sewage
landfills

1. _____ is a dangerous gas in polluted air. One source of this gas is cigarette smoke.

2. _____ is a gas that can enter buildings through cracks. It becomes trapped in the building and can cause lung cancer.

3. Any sound that is loud enough to cause harm to your ears and health is called _____.

4. _____, which includes chemical or human waste, can be harmful if dumped into a water supply.

5. _____ attract rats, insects, and rodents. These animals spread pathogens to humans.

6. _____ is particulates and products in the environment that can harm health.

7. The _____ is an office of the government that determines rules and laws to control pollution.

Write a newspaper editorial about the importance of decreasing pollution where you live. Include in your editorial at least 3 facts about pollution.

Decimals that name hundreds can easily be written as percents because <u>percent</u> means "per hundred."

Write a percent and a decimal for each picture (shaded area).

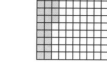

1. _____ _____

2. _____ _____

3. _____ _____

Write each percentage below as a decimal.

4. 27% = ____	5. 35% = ____	6. 54% = ____	7. 43% = ____
8. 95% = ____	9. 7% = ____	10. 18% = ____	11. 3% = ____

Write each decimal below as a percentage.

12. .15 = ____	13. .88 = ____	14. .07 = ____	15. .91 = ____
16. .05 = ____	17. .1 = ____	18. .6 = ____	19. .4 = ____

Find the number for each percentage below.

20. 8% of 45 = <u>.08</u> × <u>45</u> = <u>3.6</u>	21. 7% of 90 = ____ × ____ = ____
22. 90% of 185 = ____ × ____ = ____	23. 33% of 96 = ____ × ____ = ____

The casualties in World War I were overwhelming. Study the chart below of the number of estimated combat deaths from the major countries involved. Answer the questions below.

Allied Powers		Central Powers	
Country	**Number of Deaths**	**Country**	**Number of Deaths**
United States	.049 million	Turkey	.7 million
Italy	.5 million	Austria	1.2 million
Great Britain	1 million	Germany	1.8 million
France	1.4 million		
Russia	1.7 million		

1. Did the Allied Powers or Central Powers have more deaths? By how many?_____

2. What was the total number of estimated combat deaths in World War I?_____

3. How many more deaths did Great Britain have than the United States? _____

4. Why do you think Germany lost the most soldiers in World War I? _____

Rewrite this friendly letter using the correct form, punctuation marks, capital letters, etc. Be sure to indent at the beginning of each paragraph.

1624 bay lane short creek pa 12526 may 10 1996 dear aunt ann and uncle york school will soon be out for the summer i am looking forward to it the year has been good and i have learned a lot but it was a long one mom and dad are going to france in july i don't want to go with them i'm writing this letter to ask if i can stay with you for two weeks it would be july 10 through the 22 i would love to help you take care of the horses and do anything else you want me to do i would also help around the house please let me know if i can come your loving niece julie ann

_____

_____

_____

_____

_____

_____

_____

_____

_____

Now address the envelope for Julie Ann's letter. Be sure to put the addresses on the envelope in the right places. Put in capitals and punctuation marks.

The addresses are
mr and mrs york batty
1010 a and y ranch rt 2
box 10 ely idaho 89621
julie ann fobbs 1624 bay
lane short creek pa 12526

Mixed Practice.

1. $24.98	2. $89.82	3. 86,945	4. 3,921
14.20	42.47	6,913	1,823
10.19	8.18	7,428	4,765
+ 82.27	+ 75.03	+ 5,317	+ 5,283

5. 674	6. 5,978	7. 95.27	8. 438.5
× 392	× 703	× 5.93	× 4.86

9. 74)95,634   10. 82)809,593   11. 69)593,745   12. 93)729,374

13. $6 \frac{3}{5} \times 1 \frac{2}{8} =$ 14. $2 \frac{1}{2} \times 4 \frac{1}{5} =$

15. $2 \frac{2}{5} + 6 \frac{3}{4} =$ 16. $8 - 2 \frac{3}{4} =$

The answers are already given, but you need to come up with the questions. All the questions regard the Civil Rights Movement in the 1950s and 1960s.

1. Answer: The separation of black and white people from each other.
   Question:

2. Answer: An organization that tries to help African-Americans gain their civil rights.
   Question:

3. Answer: In 1955, she refused to give up her seat on the bus to a white passenger.
   Question:

4. Answer: A reverend who believed that African-Americans needed to protest against inequality in a nonviolent manner.
   Question:

Use these adverbs to fill in the puzzle. Use each word only once. One has been done for you.

yesterday
least
~~completely~~
carefully
loudly
slowly

almost
badly
above
yeah
yet
rapidly

impatiently
too
today
better
yonder
quickly

lightly
wildly
hardest
confidentially
lusciously
reluctantly

c o m p l e t e l y

Lung Model

Have you ever wondered how your lungs are able to breathe in and out? Try this next activity. You may learn how to save someone from choking, too.

Stuff You Need:

balloons (2 small, 1 large)   masking tape
pipettes (2)   rubber bands (large)
scissors   soda bottle (2-liter)
tubing (rubber)

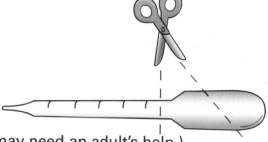

Here's What to Do:

1. Cut the pipettes as shown in the illustration. (You may need an adult's help.)

2. Place the two pipette bulbs together so that they look like the picture. You can hold them together with tape; then cut off the tops of the bulbs as shown. This will give you a "Y" connector.

3. Insert your new Y-shaped piece into the tubing and tape it in place. Attach the two small balloons to the arms of the "Y" with rubber bands.

4. Have an adult help you cut off the bottom of the 2-liter bottle.

5. Insert the tubing through the bottom of the bottle and out through the neck. Use tape to seal the tubing at the neck so that the balloons are suspended inside the bottle.

6. Cut the neck off the large balloon. Stretch the rest of the balloon over the bottom of the bottle. Use a rubber band to keep it in place.

7. Pull on the bottom balloon, but be careful not to pull it off the bottle. Watch what happens to the small balloons.

What's This All About?

The long tube at the top represents your trachea (where the air comes in). The two arms of the plastic piece represent bronchial tubes (tubes which lead to the lungs). The small balloons are the lungs. By pulling on the bottom balloon, which represents the diaphragm (a large muscle under the lungs), you lower the pressure inside the bottle (your chest cavity). This causes the balloons/lungs to inflate because the outside air pressure is now higher than the inside air pressure, and air rushes in to equalize it. When you let go of the diaphragm, you increase the inside air pressure, and the lungs deflate as the air rushes out. The diaphragm (with help from other muscles) pulls air into the lungs and then pushes it out again. While the air is inside, the lungs collect carbon dioxide out of the blood and put oxygen back into it. The carbon dioxide is then shoved out with the next exhale. It's a great system!

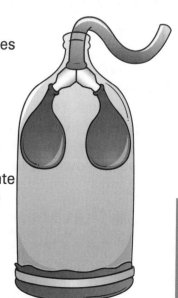

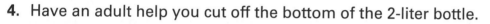

Build a Backbone

Where would you be without a backbone? You wouldn't be able to pick up your pencil if you dropped it. You wouldn't be able to sit in a chair. You wouldn't even be able to walk. Without a backbone, you wouldn't be able to do much of anything!

Stuff You Need:

hole punch
cardboard tubes (short) (11)

scissors
rubber bands (2 inches long) (11)

Here's What to Do:

1. Cut each of the cardboard tubes in thirds. If the tubes bend as you cut them, just push them back to their original shapes.

2. Punch two holes on opposite sides of each tube. Use the illustration as a guide.

3. Loop the rubber bands together to form one long string. Thread the string of rubber bands through the holes in the tube sections one at a time. When all of the sections are threaded on the rubber-band string, tie off the string at the top and bottom. You've made a backbone!

4. Experiment by bending your handmade backbone in different directions. See if your backbone has limitations and try to figure out what would happen if one or more of the sections were damaged or had to be removed.

5. Imagine that your real backbone is frozen into one solid piece for 60 seconds. Demonstrate how you would walk across the room, pick up a chair, and then put it down again. Remember, none of your vertebrae can move for 60 seconds!

What's This All About?

The backbone serves as the major supporting structure in the body, which means it must possess a lot of rigidity. At the same time, it must be flexible to allow twisting, turning, and bending. In order to accommodate this movement, the backbone is divided into sections called **vertebrae**. The human body has 33 vertebrae. They permit swaying and bending and, at the same time, provide support for the head and a place for the ribs and the hip bones to attach. Additionally, the delicate spinal cord runs through these vertebrae, with each vertebra providing openings or exit points where the spinal nerves can go to the various organs in the body.

More Fun Ideas to Try:

Compare a picture of your vertebrae to a picture of a giraffe's vertebrae and an owl's vertebrae. Which spine has the most vertebrae? Why do you think one animal might need more than another?

Answer Pages

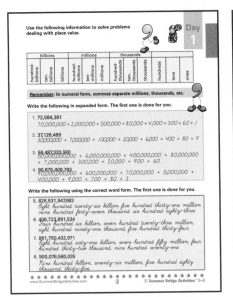

Page 3

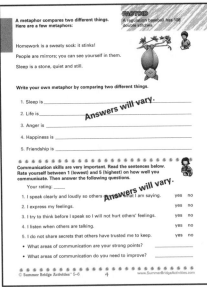

Page 4

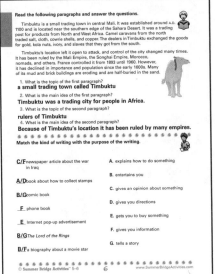

Page 5

Page 6

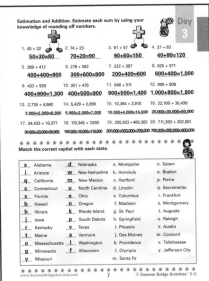

Page 7

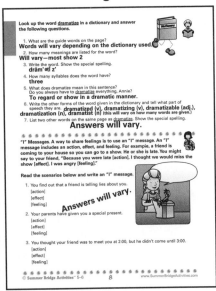

Page 8

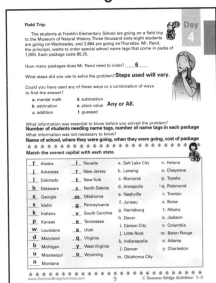

Page 9

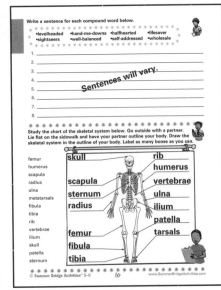

Page 10

Page 11

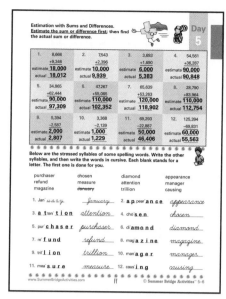

Estimation with Sums and Differences.
Estimate the sum or difference first; then find the actual sum or difference.

Day 5

1.	8,666 +9,346	2.	7,543 +2,396	3.	3,693 +1,690	4.	54,561 +36,287
estimate **18,000**		estimate **10,000**		estimate **6,000**		estimate **90,000**	
actual **18,012**		actual **9,939**		actual **5,383**		actual **90,848**	

5.	34,865 +62,444	6.	47,267 +55,085	7.	65,639 +53,263	8.	28,790 +83,964
estimate **90,000**		estimate **110,000**		estimate **120,000**		estimate **110,000**	
actual **97,309**		actual **102,352**		actual **118,902**		actual **112,754**	

9.	5,394 -2,587	10.	3,368 -2,139	11.	69,293 -22,887	12.	125,394 -69,831
estimate **2,000**		estimate **1,000**		estimate **50,000**		estimate **60,000**	
actual **2,807**		actual **1,229**		actual **46,406**		actual **55,563**	

Below are the stressed syllables of some spelling words. Write the other syllables, and then write the words in cursive. Each blank stands for a letter. The first one is done for you.

purchaser   chosen   diamond   appearance
refund   measure   attention   manager
magazine   ~~January~~ trillion   causing

1. Jan**ᵘ a r y**   *January*
2. a p·pear·**ance**   *appearance*
3. a·t**ten·tion**   *attention*
4. cho**·sen**   *chosen*
5. pur·**chaser**   *purchaser*
6. di·**amond**   *diamond*
7. re·**fund**   *refund*
8. mag·**azine**   *magazine*
9. tril·**lion**   *trillion*
10. man·**ager**   *manager*
11. mea·**sure**   *measure*
12. caus·**ing**   *causing*

Page 12

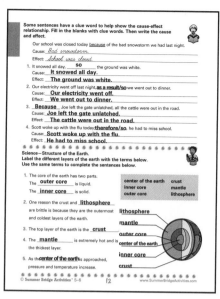

Some sentences have a clue word to help show the cause-effect relationship. Fill in the blanks with clue words. Then write the cause and effect.

Our school was closed today **because** of the bad snowstorm we had last night.
Cause: *Bad snowstorm.*
Effect: *School was closed.*

1. It snowed all day, **so** the ground was white.
   Cause: **It snowed all day.**
   Effect: **The ground was white.**
2. Our electricity went off last night, **as a result/so** we went out to dinner.
   Cause: **Our electricity went off.**
   Effect: **We went out to dinner.**
3. **Because** Joe left the gate unlatched, all the cattle were out in the road.
   Cause: **Joe left the gate unlatched.**
   Effect: **The cattle were out in the road.**
4. Scott woke up with the flu today; **therefore/so** he had to miss school.
   Cause: **Scott woke up with the flu.**
   Effect: **He had to miss school.**

Science—Structure of the Earth.
Label the different layers of the earth with the terms below.
Use the same terms to complete the sentences below.

1. The core of the earth has two parts.
   The **outer core** is liquid.
   The **inner core** is solid.

center of the earth   crust
inner core   mantle
outer core   lithosphere

2. One reason the crust and **lithosphere** are brittle is because they are the outermost and coldest layers of the earth.
3. The top layer of the earth is the **crust**
4. The **mantle** is extremely hot and is the thickest layer.
5. As the **center of the earth** is approached, pressure and temperature increase.

Labels: lithosphere, outer core, center of the earth, inner core, crust

Page 13

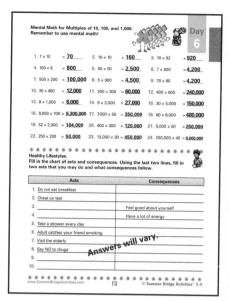

Mental Math for Multiples of 10, 100, and 1,000.
Remember to use mental math!

Day 6

1. 7 × 10 = **70**	2. 16 × 10 = **160**	3. 10 × 92 = **920**
4. 100 × 8 = **800**	5. 50 × 50 = **2,500**	6. 7 × 600 = **4,200**
7. 500 × 200 = **100,000**	8. 5 × 900 = **4,500**	9. 70 × 60 = **4,200**
10. 30 × 400 = **12,000**	11. 200 × 300 = **60,000**	12. 400 × 600 = **240,000**
13. 8 × 1,000 = **8,000**	14. 9 × 3,000 = **27,000**	15. 30 × 5,000 = **150,000**
16. 9,000 × 700 = **6,300,000**	17. 7,000 × 50 = **350,000**	18. 60 × 8,000 = **480,000**
19. 52 × 2,000 = **104,000**	20. 400 × 300 = **120,000**	21. 5,000 × 50 = **250,000**
22. 250 × 200 = **50,000**	23. 15,000 × 30 = **450,000**	24. 200,000 × 40 = **8,000,000**

Healthy Lifestyles.
Fill in the chart of acts and consequences. Using the last two lines, fill in two acts that you may do and what consequences follow.

Acts	Consequences
1. Do not eat breakfast	
2. Cheat on test	
3.	Feel good about yourself
4.	Have a lot of energy
5. Take a shower every day	
6. Adult catches your friend smoking	
7. Visit the elderly	
8. Say NO to drugs	*Answers will vary.*
9.	
10.	

Page 14

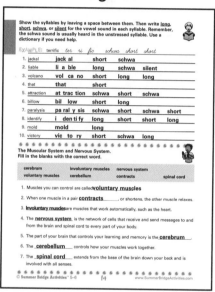

Show the syllables by leaving a space between them. Then write long, short, schwa, or silent for the vowel sound in each syllable. Remember, the schwa sound is usually heard in the unstressed syllable. Use a dictionary if you need help.

EXAMPLE: terrific   *ter ri fic*   schwa short short

1. jackal   *jack al*   short schwa
2. liable   *li a ble*   long schwa silent
3. volcano   *vol ca no*   short long long
4. that   *that*   short
5. attraction   *at trac tion*   schwa short schwa
6. billow   *bil low*   short long
7. paralysis   *pa ral y sis*   schwa short schwa short
8. identify   *i den ti fy*   long short short long
9. mold   *mold*   long
10. victory   *vic to ry*   short schwa long

The Muscular System and Nervous System.
Fill in the blanks with the correct word.

cerebrum	involuntary muscles	nervous system
voluntary muscles	cerebellum	contracts	spinal cord

1. Muscles you can control are called **voluntary muscles**
2. When one muscle in a pair **contracts**, or shortens, the other muscle relaxes.
3. **Involuntary muscles** are muscles that work automatically, such as the heart.
4. The **nervous system** is the network of cells that receive and send messages to and from the brain and spinal cord to every part of your body.
5. The part of your brain that controls your learning and memory is the **cerebrum**
6. The **cerebellum** controls how your muscles work together.
7. The **spinal cord** extends from the base of the brain down your back and is involved with all senses.

Page 15

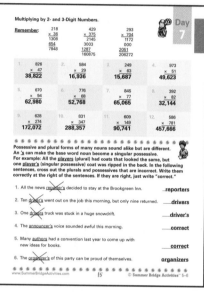

Multiplying by 2- and 3-Digit Numbers.

Day 7

Remember:
218 × 36	429 × 375	293 × 704
1308 654 7848	2145 3003 1287 160875	1172 000 2051 206272

1. 826 × 47 **38,822**	2. 584 × 29 **16,936**	3. 249 × 63 **15,687**	4. 973 × 51 **49,623**
5. 670 × 94 **62,980**	6. 776 × 68 **52,768**	7. 845 × 77 **65,065**	8. 392 × 82 **32,144**
9. 628 × 274 **172,072**	10. 831 × 347 **288,357**	11. 609 × 149 **90,741**	12. 586 × 781 **457,666**

Possessive and plural forms of many nouns sound alike but are different. An **'s** can make the base word noun become a singular possessive. For example: All the **players** (plural) had coats that looked the same, but one **player's** (singular possessive) coat was ripped in the back. In the following sentences, cross out the plurals and possessives that are incorrect. Write them correctly at the right of the sentences. If they are right, just write "correct."

1. All the news ~~reporter's~~ decided to stay at the Brookgreen Inn.   **reporters**
2. Ten ~~driver's~~ went out on the job this morning, but only nine returned.   **drivers**
3. One ~~drivers~~ truck was stuck in a huge snowdrift.   **driver's**
4. The announcer's voice sounded awful this morning.   **correct**
5. Many authors had a convention last year to come up with new ideas for books.   **correct**
6. The ~~organizer's~~ of this party can be proud of themselves.   **organizers**

Page 16

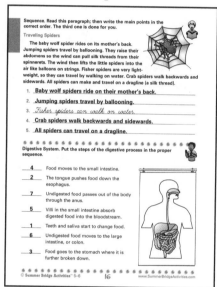

Sequence. Read this paragraph; then write the main points in the correct order. The third one is done for you.

Traveling Spiders

The baby wolf spider rides on its mother's back. Jumping spiders travel by ballooning. They raise their abdomens so the wind can pull silk threads from their spinnerets. The wind then lifts the little spiders into the air like balloons on strings. Fisher spiders are very light-weight, so they can travel by walking on water. Crab spiders walk backwards and sideways. All spiders can make and travel on a dragline (a silk thread).

1. **Baby wolf spiders ride on their mother's back.**
2. **Jumping spiders travel by ballooning.**
3. **Fisher spiders can walk on water.**
4. **Crab spiders walk backwards and sideways.**
5. **All spiders can travel on a dragline.**

Digestive System. Put the steps of the digestive process in the proper sequence.

4 Food moves to the small intestine.
2 The tongue pushes food down the esophagus.
7 Undigested food passes out of the body through the anus.
5 Villi in the small intestine absorb digested food into the bloodstream.
1 Teeth and saliva start to change food.
6 Undigested food moves to the large intestine, or colon.
3 Food goes to the stomach where it is further broken down.

Page 17

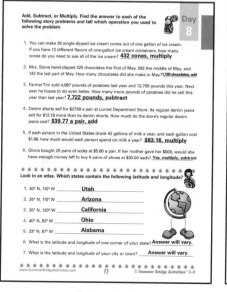

Add, Subtract, or Multiply. Find the answer to each of the following story problems and tell which operation you used to solve the problem.

Day 8

1. You can make 36 single-dipped ice cream cones out of one gallon of ice cream. If you have 12 different flavors of one-gallon ice cream containers, how many cones do you need to use all of the ice cream? **432 cones, multiply**
2. Mrs. Stone hand-dipped 425 chocolates the first of May, 592 the middle of May, and 143 the last part of May. How many chocolates did she make in May? **1,160 chocolates, add**
3. Farmer Tim sold 4,987 pounds of potatoes last year and 12,709 pounds this year. Next year he hopes to do even better. How many more pounds of potatoes did he sell this year than last year? **7,722 pounds, subtract**
4. Denim shorts sell for $27.59 a pair at Lornet Department Store. Its regular denim jeans sell for $12.18 more than its denim shorts. How much do the store's regular denim jeans cost? **$39.77 a pair, add**
5. If each person in the United States drank 42 gallons of milk a year, and each gallon cost $1.98, how much would each person spend on milk a year? **$83.16, multiply**
6. Gloria bought 25 pairs of socks at $5.80 a pair. If her mother gave her $500, would she have enough money left to buy 6 pairs of shoes at $30.00 each? **Yes, multiply, subtract**

Look in an atlas. Which states contain the following latitude and longitude?

1. 40° N, 110° W   **Utah**
2. 35° N, 110° W   **Arizona**
3. 35° N, 120° W   **California**
4. 40° N, 83° W   **Ohio**
5. 33° N, 87° W   **Alabama**
6. What is the latitude and longitude of one corner of your state? **Answer will vary.**
7. What is the latitude and longitude of your city or town? **Answer will vary.**

Page 18

Context clues help you learn new words and their meanings. Use the context clues in the following sentences to tell what the underlined words mean.

1. Mary feigned surprise when her friends had a birthday party for her.
   feigned— **pretended**
2. My colleagues and I work together on many new projects.
   colleagues— **people who work together**
3. Maurice looks at his watch often to make sure he is always punctual.
   punctual— **on time**
4. Joseph, a philatelist, has a large collection of stamps.
   philatelist— **a stamp collector**
5. The pig napping in the mud was hardly able to bestir itself for its dinner.
   bestir— **awaken**

Read the following passage and answer the questions below.

Englishman Sir Walter Raleigh wanted to start a colony in the New World (North America). In 1585, Raleigh sent colonists to what is now North Carolina. The colonists did not want to work and almost starved to death. They were taken back to England. Two years later a second group of colonists sailed over to the same place as the previous colonists. They worked very hard to survive.

Because of a war involving England, Raleigh lost track of the colonists. In 1591, a ship from England finally arrived to check on the colonists, but the colonists had disappeared! There was no sign of life. All the sailors found were some empty trunks, rotted maps, and the word CROATOAN carved on the doorpost of the fort. Croatoan was an island 100 miles south of the Lost Colony. No one knows if the colonists were attacked by the Croatoan Indians or if the settlers went to live on Croatoan Island. The Lost Colony has been a great mystery in American history.

1. How many years has it been since the first colony settled in North Carolina?
   Subtract 1585 from present year.
2. How many years did it take to send a ship to check on the second set of colonists?
   4 years
3. Why was this colony called the Lost Colony?
   No one knows what happened to the settlers.
4. State what you think might have happened to the Lost Colony.
   Answer will vary.
5. Think of a title that would be appropriate for this passage.
   Answer will vary.

Page 19

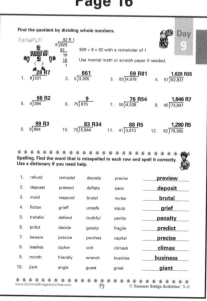

Find the quotient by dividing whole numbers.

Day 9

EXAMPLE:
```
     92 R 1
  9)829
    81
    19
    18
     1
```
829 ÷ 9 = 92 with a remainder of 1
Use mental math or scratch paper if needed.

1. 8)231 **28 R7**	2. 5)3,305 **661**	3. 83)4,978 **59 R81**	4. 57)92,831 **1,628 R35**
5. 4)394 **98 R2**	6. 75)675 **9**	7. 59)4,538 **76 R54**	8. 40)73,847 **1,846 R7**
9. 9)894 **99 R3**	10. 70)5,844 **83 R34**	11. 41)3,613 **88 R5**	12. 62)79,365 **1,280 R5**

Spelling. Find the word that is misspelled in each row and spell it correctly. Use a dictionary if you need help.

1.	refund	remodel	decode	previw	**preview**
2.	deposet	pretend	deflate	pace	**deposit**
3.	mold	respond	brutel	revise	**brutal**
4.	fiction	grieff	unsafe	equip	**grief**
5.	transfer	defend	truthful	penlty	**penalty**
6.	prdict	decide	gossip	fragile	**predict**
7.	beware	precice	porches	capital	**precise**
8.	leashes	cipher	volt	climack	**climax**
9.	month	friendly	wrench	businss	**business**
10.	jiant	angle	guest	greet	**giant**

Page 20

Remember: Prefixes are added to the beginning of base words. Add prefixes to these base words. Use as many prefixes as you can with the base words and see how many words you can make. Use prefixes *mis-*, *re-*, *un-*, *non-*, and *pre-*.

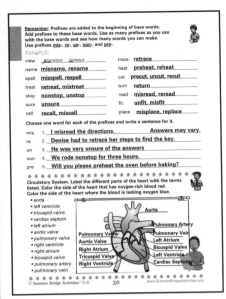

EXAMPLE:

view	_preview, review_	trace	**retrace**
name	**misname, rename**	heat	**preheat, reheat**
spell	**misspell, respell**	cut	**precut, uncut, recut**
treat	**retreat, mistreat**	turn	**return**
stop	**nonstop, unstop**	read	**misread, reread**
sure	**unsure**	fit	**unfit, misfit**
call	**recall, miscall**	place	**misplace, replace**

Choose one word for each of the prefixes and write a sentence for each.

mis 1. **I misread the directions.** Answers may vary.
re   2. **Denise had to retrace her steps to find the key.**
un   3. **He was very unsure of the answers**
non 4. **We rode nonstop for three hours.**
pre 5. **Will you please preheat the oven before baking?**

Circulatory System. Label the different parts of the heart with the terms listed. Color the side of the heart that has oxygen-rich blood red. Color the side of the heart where the blood is lacking oxygen blue.

- aorta
- left ventricle
- tricuspid valve
- cardiac septum
- left atrium
- aortic valve
- pulmonary valve
- right ventricle
- right atrium
- bicuspid valve
- pulmonary artery
- pulmonary vein

Aorta

Pulmonary Valve — Pulmonary Artery
Aortic Valve — Pulmonary Vein
Right Atrium — Left Atrium
Tricuspid Valve — Bicuspid Valve
Right Ventricle — Left Ventricle
— Cardiac Septum

© Summer Bridge Activities™ 5–6   20   www.SummerBridgeActivities.com

---

Page 21

Day 10

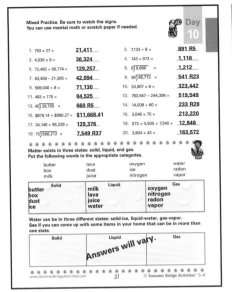

Mixed Practice. Be sure to watch the signs. You can use mental math or scratch paper if needed.

1. 793 × 27 =   **21,411**
2. 7,133 ÷ 8 =   **891 R5**
3. 4,036 × 9 =   **36,324**
4. 143 + 973 =   **1,116**
5. 72,483 + 56,774 = **129,257**
6. 8)9,696 =   **1,212**
7. 63,459 − 21,365 = **42,094**
8. 90)48,713 =   **541 R23**
9. 569,040 + 8 =   **71,130**
10. 53,907 × 6 =   **323,442**
11. 483 × 175 =   **84,525**
12. 763,947 − 244,398 = **519,549**
13. 45)29,705 =   **660 R5**
14. 14,008 ÷ 60 =   **233 R28**
15. $678.14 + $990.27 = **$11,668.41**
16. 3,046 × 70 =   **213,220**
17. 34,148 + 95,228 = **129,376**
18. 573 + 4,935 + 7,340 = **12,848**
19. 75)566,212 =   **7,549 R37**
20. 3,804 × 43 =   **163,572**

Matter exists in three states: solid, liquid, and gas. Put the following words in the appropriate categories.

butter	lava	oxygen	water
box	dust	ice	radon
milk	juice	nitrogen	vapor

Solid	Liquid	Gas
butter	**milk**	**oxygen**
box	**lava**	**nitrogen**
dust	**juice**	**radon**
ice	**water**	**vapor**

Water can be in three different states: solid-ice, liquid-water, gas-vapor. See if you can come up with some items in your home that can be in more than one state.

Solid	Liquid	Gas
	Answers will vary.	

www.SummerBridgeActivities.com   21   © Summer Bridge Activities™ 5–6

Page 22

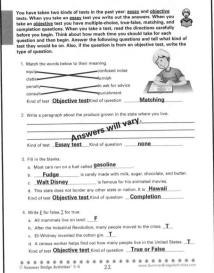

You have taken two kinds of tests in the past year: **essay** and **objective** tests. When you take an **essay** test you write out the answers. When you take an **objective** test you have multiple-choice, true-false, matching, and completion questions. When you take a test, read the directions carefully before you begin. Think about how much time you should take for each question and then begin. Answer the following questions and tell what kind of test they would be on. Also, if the question is from an objective test, write the type of question.

1. Match the words below to their meaning.

equip — confused noise
clatter — furnish
penalty — to ask for advice
consult — punishment

Kind of test **Objective test** Kind of question **Matching**

2. Write a paragraph about the produce grown in the state where you live.

_____

Answers will vary.

Kind of test **Essay test** Kind of question **none**

3. Fill in the blanks.
   a. Most cars run on a fuel called **gasoline** .
   b. **Fudge** is candy made with milk, sugar, chocolate, and butter.
   c. **Walt Disney** is famous for his animated movies.
   d. This state does not border any other state or nation. It is **Hawaii** .
   Kind of test **Objective test** Kind of question **Completion**

4. Write **F** for false, **T** for true.
   a. All mammals live on land. **F**
   b. After the Industrial Revolution, many people moved to the cities. **T**
   c. Eli Whitney invented the cotton gin. **T**
   d. A census worker helps find out how many people live in the United States. **T**
   Kind of test **Objective test** Kind of question **True or False**

© Summer Bridge Activities™ 5–6   22   www.SummerBridgeActivities.com

---

Page 23

Day 11

Multiples and Common Multiples.

Remember: A **multiple** is a number exactly divisible by another number. 6 12 18 24 30 are multiples of 6.

List 5 or 6 multiples for the following numbers.

1. 5 **10 15 20 25 30 35**
2. 10 **20 30 40 50 60 70**
3. 9 **18 27 36 45 54 63**
4. 12 **24 36 48 60 72 84**
5. 3 **6 9 12 15 18 21**
6. 2 **4 6 7 10 12 14**

Remember: The common multiples for 2 and 4 are 4, 8, 12, or "other numbers in common."

List 3 common multiples for these numbers.

7. 3 and 4 **12 24 36**
8. 4 and 7 **28 56 84**
9. 5 and 10 **20 30 40**
10. 6 and 8 **24 48 72**
11. 2 and 9 **18 36 54**
12. 5 and 6 **30 60 90**
13. What is the least common multiple for 2 and 9? **18**
14. For 5 and 6? **30** 15. For 3 and 4? **12** 16. For 8 and 10? **40**

Refusal skills help a person say NO to risky behaviors and situations. Here are some refusal skills you can use:

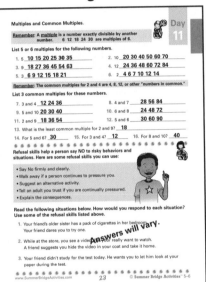

- Say No firmly and clearly.
- Walk away if a person continues to pressure you.
- Suggest an alternative activity.
- Tell an adult you trust if you are continually pressured.
- Explain the consequences.

Read the following situations below. How would you respond to each situation? Use some of the refusal skills listed above.

1. Your friend's older sister has a pack of cigarettes in her bedroom. Your friend dares you to try one.

2. While at the store, you see a video game you really want to watch. A friend suggests you hide the video in your coat and take it home.

3. Your friend didn't study for the test today. He wants you to let him look at your paper during the test.

Answers will vary.

www.SummerBridgeActivities.com   23   © Summer Bridge Activities™ 5–6

Page 24

Writing Complete Sentences. **Remember:** A complete sentence expresses a complete thought. If it does not express a complete thought it is called a sentence fragment. A complete sentence needs to tell whom or what the sentence is about and what happened to the whom or what.

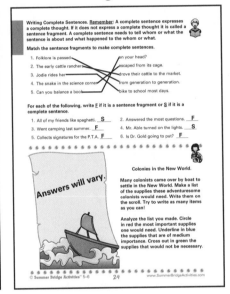

Match the sentence fragments to make complete sentences.

1. Folklore is passed — on your head?
2. The early cattle ranchers — escaped from its cage.
3. Jodie rides her — drove their cattle to the market.
4. The snake in the science corner — from generation to generation.
5. Can you balance a book — bike to school most days.

For each of the following, write **F** if it is a sentence fragment or **S** if it is a complete sentence.

1. All of my friends like spaghetti. **S**
2. Answered the most questions. **F**
3. Went camping last summer. **F**
4. Mr. Able turned on the lights. **S**
5. Collects signatures for the P.T.A. **F**
6. Is Dr. Gold going to put? **F**

Colonies in the New World.

Many colonists came over by boat to settle in the New World. Make a list of the supplies these adventuresome colonists would need. Write them on the scroll. Try to write as many items as you can!

Analyze the list you made. Circle in red the most important supplies one would need. Underline in blue the supplies that are of medium importance. Cross out in green the supplies that would not be necessary.

Answers will vary.

© Summer Bridge Activities™ 5–6   24   www.SummerBridgeActivities.com

---

Page 25

Day 12

Remember: The first step when adding or subtracting decimals is to line up the decimals. If the number of decimal places is not the same, you can attach zeros to the end of a number to make it easier.

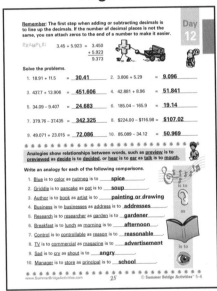

EXAMPLE: 3.45 + 5.923 → 3.450 + 5.923 = 9.373

Solve the problems.

1. 18.91 + 11.5 = **30.41**
2. 3.806 + 5.29 = **9.096**
3. 437.7 + 13.906 = **451.606**
4. 42.881 + 8.96 = **51.841**
5. 34.09 − 9.407 = **24.683**
6. 185.04 − 165.9 = **19.14**
7. 379.76 − 37.435 = **342.325**
8. $224.00 − $116.98 = **$107.02**
9. 49.071 + 23.015 = **72.086**
10. 85.089 − 34.12 = **50.969**

Analogies show relationships between words, such as **preview** is to **previewed** as **decide** is to **decided**, or **hear** is to **ear** as **talk** is to **mouth**.

Write an analogy for each of the following comparisons.

1. Blue is to color as nutmeg is to **spice** .
2. Griddle is to pancake as pot is to **soup** .
3. Author is to book as artist is to **painting or drawing** .
4. Business is to businesses as address is to **addresses** .
5. Research is to researcher as garden is to **gardener** .
6. Breakfast is to lunch as morning is to **afternoon** .
7. Control is to controllable as reason is to **reasonable** .
8. TV is to commercial as magazine is to **advertisement** .
9. Sad is to cry as shout is to **angry** .
10. Manager is to store as principal is to **school** .

www.SummerBridgeActivities.com   25   © Summer Bridge Activities™ 5–6

Page 26

A **subject** tells what or whom the sentence is about. A **predicate** tells about the subject.

Subject   Predicate

Listed below are some predicates. Write a complete subject to go with them.

1. **The game / Magic tricks** fascinated Megan.
2. **All living things** need water.
3. **The huge building** collapsed suddenly.
4. **John / My father** misplaced his new watch.
5. **The students /The girls** know how to operate the computers.

Listed below are some complete subjects. Write a complete predicate to go with them.

6. The package **was huge and bulky / was lost in the mail**
7. A team of horses **pulled the wagons / sold for $2,000.00**
8. The famous actress **won many awards / performed in five plays last year**
9. Sarah and Julie **went for a plane ride / visited their grandmother**
10. Anthills **can be found in many places / are the homes for ants**

Answers will vary.

An **entry word** is a word you look up in the dictionary. It is the simplest form of the word. If you want to find out what *costly* means, you would look up the word *cost* in the dictionary.

What would the entry word be for each of these words?

1. celebrated _celebrate_
2. happier   **happy**
3. chilly   **chill**
4. classical   **classic**
5. faster   **fast**
6. couples   **couple**
7. deformed   **deform**

© Summer Bridge Activities™ 5–6   26   www.SummerBridgeActivities.com

---

Page 27

Day 13

Multiplying Whole Numbers and Decimals. Remember to put the decimal point in the correct place in the product.

1. 0.12 × 6 = **.72**
2. 0.08 × 7 = **.56**
3. 4.6 × 3 = **13.8**
4. 5.05 × 8 = **40.40**
5. 6.5 × 13 = **84.5**
6. 1.906 × 28 = **53.368**
7. 7.0216 × 52 = **365.1232**
8. 6.65 × 77 = **512.05**
9. 5.364 × 93 = **498.852**
10. 359.073 × 24 = **8,617.752**
11. 5.9081 × 71 = **419.4751**
12. 12.504 × 99 = **1,237.896**
13. 8.709 × 56 = **487.704**
14. 27.035 × 93 = **2,514.255**

15. Jan works delivering pizza and gets paid $37.40 a night. She works 23 nights each month. How much does Jan earn each month? **$860.20**

16. Jake works at a grocery store. He gets paid $8.65 an hour for each hour he works. He usually works 37 hours a week. How much does he earn in a week? **$320.05** How much would he earn in 4 weeks? **$1,280.20**

Find the next number in the number patterns below.

1. 4, 8, 16, 32, 64, **128**
2. 1, 4, 7, 6, 9, 12, 11, **14**
3. 1, 4, 7, 10, 13, 16, **19**
4. 3, 6, 5, 10, 8, 16, 13, 13, **26**
5. 3, 5, 8, 12, 17, 23, **30**
6. 0, 1, 2, 3, 4, 5, 6, 7, 8, 9, 10, **11**
7. 6, 36, 66, 96, **126**
8. 1, 1, 1, 3, 2, 2, 6, 5, 5, 15, 14, 14, **42**

www.SummerBridgeActivities.com   27   © Summer Bridge Activities™ 5–6

Page 28

Two Kinds of Verbs: Action Verbs and State-of-Being Verbs.

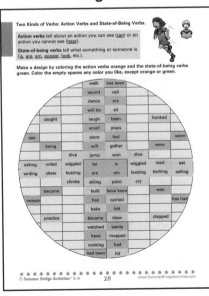

Action verbs tell about an action you can see (*ran*) or an action you cannot see (*hear*).

State-of-being verbs tell what something or someone is (*is*, *are*, *am*, *appear*, *look*, etc.).

Make a design by coloring the action verbs orange and the state-of-being verbs green. Color the empty spaces any color you like, except orange or green.

	walk	has been		
	sound	call		
	dance	are		
	will be	sit		
caught	laugh	been		honked
	smell	plays		
see	wore	feel		seem
being	will	gather		were
dive	jump	won	dive	
asking	rolled	wiggled	be	is	wiggled	read	eat
writing	cheer	buzzing	are	am	buzzing	barking	selling
	climbs	skiing	paint	cry			
become		built	have been		was		
remain		has	carried			has had	
		bake	felt				
practice		became	blew		clapped		
	watched	wants					
	have	mopped					
	cooking	had					
	had been	hit					

© Summer Bridge Activities™ 5–6   28   www.SummerBridgeActivities.com

---

Page 29

Measuring with Metrics.

1 centimeter = 10 millimeters	1 meter = 10 decimeters
1 decimeter = 10 centimeters	1 meter = 100 centimeters
1 decimeter = 100 millimeters	1 meter = 1,000 millimeters
	1 kilometer = 1,000 meters

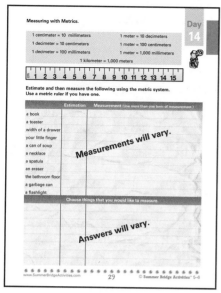

Estimate and then measure the following using the metric system. Use a metric ruler if you have one.

	Estimation	Measurement (Use more than one term of measurement.)
a book		
a toaster		
width of a drawer		
your little finger	*Measurements will vary.*	
a can of soup		
a necklace		
a spatula		
an eraser		
the bathroom floor		
a garbage can		
a flashlight		

Choose things that you would like to measure.

Answers will vary.

Page 30

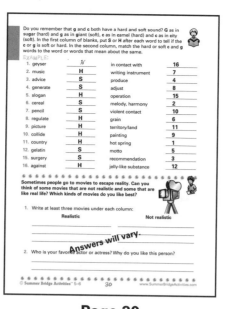

Do you remember that **g** and **c** both have a hard and soft sound? **G** as in sugar (hard) and **g** as in giant (soft), **c** as in camel (hard) and **c** as in city (soft). In the first column of blanks, put **S** or **H** after each word to tell if the **c** or **g** is soft or hard. In the second column, match the hard or soft **c** and **g** words to the word or words that mean about the same.

EXAMPLE:

1. geyser	H	in contact with	16
2. music	H	writing instrument	7
3. advice	S	produce	4
4. generate	S	adjust	8
5. slogan	H	operation	15
6. cereal	S	melody, harmony	2
7. pencil	S	violent contact	10
8. regulate	H	grain	6
9. picture	H	territory/land	11
10. collide	H	painting	9
11. country	H	hot spring	1
12. gelatin	S	motto	5
15. surgery	S	recommendation	3
16. against	H	jelly-like substance	12

Sometimes people go to movies to escape reality. Can you think of some movies that are not realistic and some that are like real life? Which kinds of movies do you like best?

1. Write at least three movies under each column:

Realistic	Not realistic

Answers will vary.

2. Who is your favorite actor or actress? Why do you like this person?

Page 31

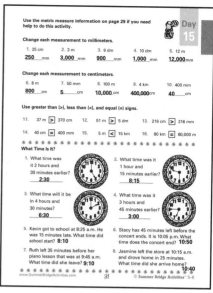

Use the metric measure information on page 29 if you need help to do this activity.

Change each measurement to millimeters.

1. 25 cm	2. 3 m	3. 9 dm	4. 10 dm	5. 12 m
250 mm	**3,000** mm	**900** mm	**1,000** mm	**12,000** mm

Change each measurement to centimeters.

6. 8 m	7. 50 mm	8. 100 m	9. 4 km	10. 400 mm
800 cm	**5** cm	**10,000** cm	**400,000** cm	**40** cm

Use greater than (>), less than (<), and equal (=) signs.

11. 37 m **>** 370 cm	12. 51 m **>** 5 dm	13. 216 cm **>** 216 mm
14. 40 cm **=** 400 mm	15. 5 m **<** 15 km	16. 80 km **=** 80,000 m

What Time Is It?

1. What time was it 2 hours and 30 minutes earlier? **2:30**

2. What time was it 1 hour and 15 minutes earlier? **8:15**

3. What time will it be in 4 hours and 30 minutes? **6:30**

4. What time was it 3 hours and 45 minutes earlier? **3:00**

5. Kevin got to school at 8:25 a.m. He was 15 minutes late. What time did school start? **8:10**

6. Stacy has 45 minutes left before the concert ends. It is 10:05 p.m. What time does the concert end? **10:50**

7. Ruth left 35 minutes before her piano lesson that was at 9:45 a.m. What time did she leave? **9:10**

8. Jasmine left the store at 10:15 a.m. and drove home in 25 minutes. What time did she arrive home? **10:40**

Page 32

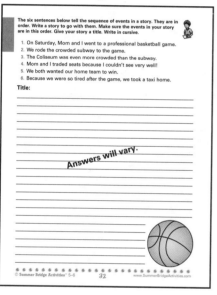

The six sentences below tell the sequence of events in a story. They are in order. Write a story to go with them. Make sure the events in your story are in this order. Give your story a title. Write in cursive.

1. On Saturday, Mom and I went to a professional basketball game.
2. We rode the crowded subway to the game.
3. The Coliseum was even more crowded than the subway.
4. Mom and I traded seats because I couldn't see very well!
5. We both wanted our home team to win.
6. Because we were so tired after the game, we took a taxi home.

Title:

Answers will vary.

Section 2

Page 37

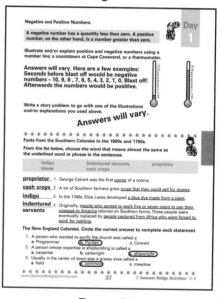

Negative and Positive Numbers.

A negative number has a quantity less than zero. A positive number, on the other hand, is a number greater than zero.

Illustrate and/or explain positive and negative numbers using a number line, a countdown at Cape Canaveral, or a thermometer.

Answers will vary. Here are a few examples: Seconds before blast off would be negative numbers – 10, 9, 8, 7, 6, 5, 4, 3, 2, 1, 0, Blast off! Afterwards the numbers would be positive.

Write a story problem to go with one of the illustrations and/or explanations you used above.

Answers will vary.

Facts from the Southern Colonies in the 1600s and 1700s.

From the list below, choose the word that means almost the same as the underlined word or phrase in the sentences.

indigo	indentured servants	proprietor
slaves	cash crops	

proprietor 1. George Calvert was the first <u>owner of a colony</u>.

cash crops 2. A lot of Southern farmers grew <u>crops that they could sell for money</u>.

indigo 3. In the 1740s, Eliza Lucas developed <u>a blue dye made from a plant</u>.

indentured servants 4. Originally, <u>people who agreed to work five or seven years to pay their passage to America</u> labored on Southern farms. These people were eventually replaced by <u>people captured from Africa who were forced to work for nothing</u>.

The New England Colonies. Circle the correct answer to complete each statement.

1. A person who wanted to purify the church was called a
   a. Programmer   **b. Puritan**   c. Convert
2. A person whose expertise is shipbuilding is called a
   a. carpenter   b. cartwright   **c. shipwright**
3. Usually in the center of town was a grassy area called a
   a. field   **b. common**   c. meadow

Page 38

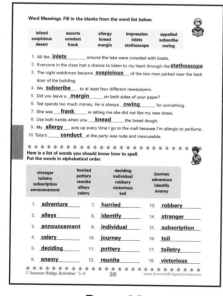

Word Meanings. Fill in the blanks from the word list below.

inland	escorts	allergy	impression	appalled
suspicious	conduct	knead	subscribe	owing
desert	frank	margin	stethoscope	

1. All the **inlets** around the lake were crowded with boats.
2. Everyone in the class had a chance to listen to my heart through the **stethoscope**.
3. The night watchman became **suspicious** of the two men parked near the back door of the building.
4. We **subscribe** to at least four different newspapers.
5. Did you leave a **margin** on both sides of your paper?
6. Ted spends too much money. He is always **owing** for something.
7. She was **frank** in telling me she did not like my new dress.
8. Use both hands when you **knead** the bread dough.
9. My **allergy** acts up every time I go to the mall because I'm allergic to perfume.
10. Toby's **conduct** at the party was rude and inexcusable.

Here is a list of words you should know how to spell. Put the words in alphabetical order.

stranger	hurried	deciding	journey
toiletry	pottery	individual	adventure
subscription	reunite	robbery	identify
announcement	alleys	victorious	enemy
	celery	toil	

1. **adventure**	7. **hurried**	13. **robbery**
2. **alleys**	8. **identify**	14. **stranger**
3. **announcement**	9. **individual**	15. **subscription**
4. **celery**	10. **journey**	16. **toil**
5. **deciding**	11. **pottery**	17. **toiletry**
6. **enemy**	12. **reunite**	18. **victorious**

Page 39

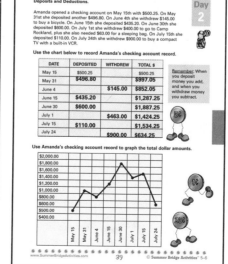

Deposits and Deductions.

Amanda opened a checking account on May 15th with $500.25. On May 31st she deposited another $496.80. On June 4th she withdrew $145.00 to buy a bicycle. On June 15th she deposited $435.20. On June 30th she deposited $600.00. On July 1st she withdrew $400.00 to go to Camp Rockland, plus she also needed $63.00 for a sleeping bag. On July 15th she deposited $110.00. On July 24th she withdrew $900.00 to buy a compact TV with a built-in VCR.

Use the chart below to record Amanda's checking account record.

DATE	DEPOSITED	WITHDREW	TOTAL $
May 15	$500.25		$500.25
May 31	$496.80		$997.05
June 4		$145.00	$852.05
June 15	$435.20		$1,287.25
June 30	$600.00		$1,887.25
July 1		$463.00	$1,424.25
July 15	$110.00		$1,534.25
July 24		$900.00	$634.25

Remember: When you deposit money you add, and when you withdraw money you subtract.

Use Amanda's checking account record to graph the total dollar amounts.

$2,000.00	
$1,800.00	
$1,600.00	
$1,400.00	
$1,200.00	
$1,000.00	
$800.00	
$600.00	
$500.00	
$400.00	

May 15, May 31, June 4, June 15, June 30, July 1, July 15, July 24

Page 40

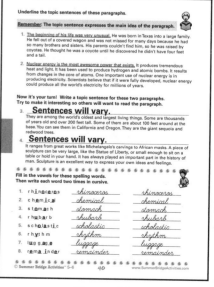

Underline the topic sentences of these paragraphs.

Remember: The topic sentence expresses the main idea of the paragraph.

1. <u>The beginning of his life was very unusual.</u> He was born in Texas into a large family. He fell out of a covered wagon and was not missed for many days because he had so many brothers and sisters. His parents couldn't find him, so he was raised by coyotes. He thought he was a coyote until he discovered he didn't have four feet and a tail.

2. <u>Nuclear energy is the most awesome power that exists.</u> It produces tremendous heat and light. It has been used to produce hydrogen and atomic bombs. It results from changes in the core of atoms. One important use of nuclear energy is in producing electricity. Scientists believe that if it were fully developed, nuclear energy could produce all the world's electricity for millions of years.

Now it's your turn! Write a topic sentence for these two paragraphs. Try to make it interesting so others will want to read the paragraph.

3. **Sentences will vary.** They are among the world's oldest and largest living things. Some are thousands of years old and over 200 feet tall. Some of them are about 100 feet around at the base. You can see them in California and Oregon. They are the giant sequoia and redwood trees.

4. **Sentences will vary.** It ranges from great works like Michelangelo's carvings to African masks. A piece of sculpture can be very large, like the Statue of Liberty, or small enough to sit on a table or hold in your hand. It has always played an important part in the history of man. Sculpture is an excellent way to express your own ideas and feelings.

Fill in the vowels for these spelling words. Then write each word two times in cursive.

1. rhinoceros	*rhinoceros*	*rhinoceros*
2. chemical	*chemical*	*chemical*
3. stomach	*stomach*	*stomach*
4. rhubarb	*rhubarb*	*rhubarb*
5. scholastic	*scholastic*	*scholastic*
6. rhythm	*rhythm*	*rhythm*
7. luggage	*luggage*	*luggage*
8. remainder	*remainder*	*remainder*

Page 41

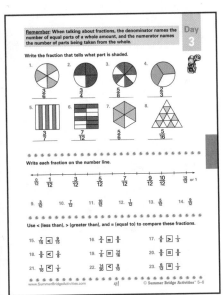

Remember: When talking about fractions, the denominator names the number of equal parts of a whole amount, and the numerator names the number of parts being taken from the whole.

Day 3

Write the fraction that tells what part is shaded.

1. $\frac{3}{6}$ 2. $\frac{3}{4}$ 3. $\frac{5}{8}$ 4. $\frac{2}{3}$

5. $\frac{3}{7}$ 6. $\frac{7}{12}$ 7. $\frac{5}{6}$ 8. $\frac{5}{16}$

Write each fraction on the number line.

$\frac{0}{12} \quad \frac{1}{12} \quad \frac{3}{12} \quad \frac{5}{12} \quad \frac{7}{12} \quad \frac{9}{12} \quad \frac{10}{12}$ or 1

9. $\frac{3}{12}$ 10. $\frac{7}{12}$ 11. $\frac{2}{12}$ 12. $\frac{1}{12}$ 13. $\frac{5}{12}$ 14. $\frac{9}{12}$

Use < (less than), > (greater than), and = (equal to) to compare these fractions.

15. $\frac{7}{15}$ < $\frac{5}{6}$ 16. $\frac{2}{4}$ = $\frac{6}{8}$ 17. $\frac{4}{6}$ > $\frac{1}{3}$

18. $\frac{5}{8}$ < $\frac{6}{8}$ 19. $\frac{7}{8}$ = $\frac{14}{16}$ 20. $\frac{3}{8}$ > $\frac{2}{9}$

21. $\frac{1}{10}$ < $\frac{1}{2}$ 22. $\frac{14}{15}$ > $\frac{8}{9}$ 23. $\frac{6}{12}$ = $\frac{1}{2}$

41

Page 42

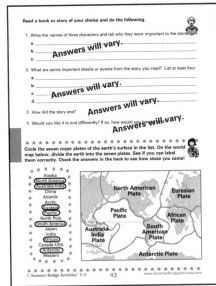

Read a book or story of your choice and do the following.

1. Write the names of three characters and tell why they were important to the story.
   a. _Answers will vary._
   b.
   c.

2. What are some important details or events from the story you read? List at least four.
   a.
   b. _Answers will vary._
   c.
   d.

3. How did the story end? _Answers will vary._

4. Would you like it to end differently? If so, how would you have it end? _Answers will vary._

Circle the seven major plates of the earth's surface in the list. On the world map below, divide the earth into the seven plates. See if you can label them correctly. Check the answers in the back to see how close you came!

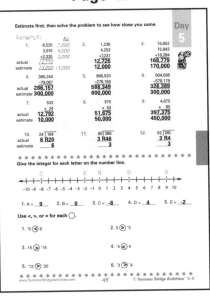

Alaska
(North America)
(Australia-India)
China
Atlantic
Arctic
(Eurasia)
(Pacific)
North Pole
(South America)
Japan
India
(Africa)
Canada-USA
(Antarctic)
Western

42

Page 43

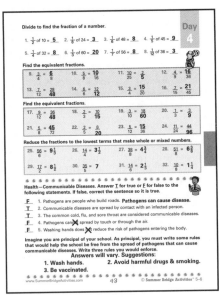

Day 4

Divide to find the fraction of a number.

1. $\frac{1}{2}$ of 10 = **5**   2. $\frac{1}{8}$ of 24 = **3**   3. $\frac{1}{6}$ of 48 = **8**   4. $\frac{1}{5}$ of 45 = **9**

5. $\frac{1}{4}$ of 32 = **8**   6. $\frac{1}{3}$ of 60 = **20**   7. $\frac{1}{7}$ of 56 = **8**   8. $\frac{1}{12}$ of 36 = **3**

Find the equivalent fractions.

9. $\frac{3}{4} = \frac{6}{8}$ 10. $\frac{5}{8} = \frac{10}{16}$ 11. $\frac{10}{25} = \frac{2}{5}$ 12. $\frac{4}{9} = \frac{16}{36}$

13. $\frac{7}{6} = \frac{28}{24}$ 14. $\frac{3}{6} = \frac{6}{12}$ 15. $\frac{5}{4} = \frac{15}{12}$ 16. $\frac{7}{15} = \frac{21}{45}$

Find the equivalent fractions.

17. $\frac{9}{12} = \frac{6}{48}$ 18. $\frac{2}{3} = \frac{10}{15}$ 19. $\frac{3}{10} = \frac{18}{60}$ 20. $\frac{1}{3} = \frac{3}{9}$

21. $\frac{5}{8} = \frac{45}{72}$ 22. $\frac{2}{5} = \frac{8}{20}$ 23. $\frac{5}{12} = \frac{15}{36}$ 24. $\frac{11}{24} = \frac{44}{96}$

Reduce the fractions to the lowest terms that make whole or mixed numbers.

25. $\frac{56}{6} = 9\frac{1}{3}$ 26. $\frac{14}{4} = 3\frac{1}{2}$ 27. $\frac{28}{8} = 3\frac{1}{2}$ 28. $\frac{51}{8} = 6\frac{3}{8}$

29. $\frac{17}{2} = 8\frac{1}{2}$ 30. $\frac{35}{5} = 7$ 31. $\frac{14}{6} = 2\frac{1}{3}$ 32. $\frac{10}{8} = 1\frac{1}{4}$

Health—Communicable Diseases. Answer T for true or F for false to the following statements. If false, correct the sentence so it is true.

F 1. Pathogens are people who build roads. _Pathogens can cause disease._

T 2. Communicable diseases are spread by contact with an infected person.

T 3. The common cold, flu, and sore throat are considered communicable diseases.

T 4. Pathogens can spread by touch or through the air.

F 5. Washing hands does not reduce the risk of pathogens entering the body.

Imagine you are principal of your school. As principal, you must write some rules that would help the school be free from the spread of pathogens that can cause communicable diseases. Write three rules you would enforce.
Answers will vary. Suggestions:
1. Wash hands.   2. Avoid harmful drugs & smoking.
3. Be vaccinated.

43

Page 44

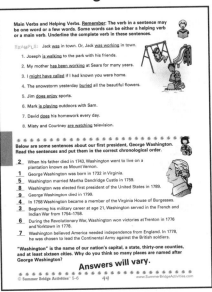

Main Verbs and Helping Verbs. **Remember:** The verb in a sentence may be one word or a few words. Some words can be either a helping verb or a main verb. Underline the complete verb in these sentences.

EXAMPLE: Jack _was_ in town. Or, Jack _was working_ in town.

1. Joseph _is walking_ to the park with his friends.

2. My mother _has been working_ at Sears for many years.

3. I _might have called_ if I had known you were home.

4. The snowstorm yesterday _buried_ all the beautiful flowers.

5. Jim _does enjoy_ sports.

6. Mark _is playing_ outdoors with Sam.

7. David _does_ his homework every day.

8. Misty and Courtney _are watching_ television.

Below are some sentences about our first president, George Washington. Read the sentences and put them in the correct chronological order.

2 When his father died in 1743, Washington went to live on a plantation known as Mount Vernon.

1 George Washington was born in 1732 in Virginia.

5 Washington married Martha Dandridge Custis in 1759.

8 Washington was elected first president of the United States in 1789.

9 George Washington died in 1799.

4 In 1758 Washington became a member of the Virginia House of Burgesses.

3 Beginning his military career at age 21, Washington served in the French and Indian War from 1754–1758.

6 During the Revolutionary War, Washington won victories at Trenton in 1776 and Yorktown in 1778.

7 Washington believed America needed independence from England. In 1778, he was chosen to lead the Continental Army against the British soldiers.

"Washington" is the name of our nation's capital, a state, thirty-one counties, and at least sixteen cities. Why do you think so many places are named after George Washington? _Answers will vary._

44

Page 45

Day 5

Estimate first; then solve the problem to see how close you came.

EXAMPLE:

	Est.
6,525	7,000
3,910	4,000
+2,335	2,000
actual 12,770	estimate 13,000 / 13,000

1. (as above)

2. 1,236 / 4,253 / +7,237 ; actual 12,726 ; estimate 12,000

3. 74,652 / 75,843 / +18,284 ; actual 168,779 ; estimate 170,000

4. 365,244 / –79,087 ; actual 286,157 ; estimate 300,000

5. 866,533 / –278,184 ; actual 588,349 ; estimate 600,000

6. 904,568 / –578,179 ; actual 326,389 ; estimate 300,000

7. 533 / x 24 ; actual 12,792 ; estimate 10,000

8. 975 / x 53 ; actual 51,675 ; estimate 50,000

9. 4,675 / x 85 ; actual 397,375 ; estimate 450,000

10. 24)164 ; actual 6 R20 ; estimate 6

11. 80)286 ; actual 3 R46 ; estimate 3

12. 62)190 ; actual 3 R4 ; estimate 3

Give the integer for each letter on the number line.

C   E   B D   A

–10 –9 –8 –7 –6 –5 –4 –3 –2 –1 0 1 2 3 4 5 6 7 8 9 10

1. A = **9**   2. B = **0**   3. C = **-8**   4. D = **4**   5. E = **-2**

Use <, >, or = for each ( ).

1. ⁻8 < 8   2. 0 > ⁻3

3. 15 > ⁻16   4. ⁻4 < 4

5. ⁻12 > ⁻20   6. ⁻3 > ⁻4

45

Page 46

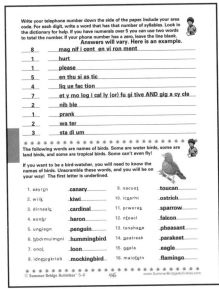

Write your telephone number down the side of the paper. Include your area code. For each digit, write a word that has that number of syllables. Look in the dictionary for help. If you have numerals over 5 you can use two words to total the number. If your phone number has a zero, leave the line blank.
Answers will vary. Here is an example.

8	mag nif i cent en vi ron ment
1	hurt
1	please
5	en thu si as tic
4	liq ue fac tion
7	et y mo log i cal ly (or) fu gi tive AND gig a cy cle
2	nib ble
1	prank
2	wa ter
3	sta di um

The following words are names of birds. Some are water birds, some are land birds, and some are tropical birds. Some can't even fly!

If you want to be a bird-watcher, you will need to know the names of birds. Unscramble these words, and you will be on your way! The first letter is underlined.

1. aayrcn   **canary**   9. nacuot   **toucan**
2. wiik   **kiwi**   10. icgarht   **ostrich**
3. dirnaalc **cardinal**   11. prworas   **sparrow**
4. eonhr   **heron**   12. nfoacl   **falcon**
5. unpiegn   **penguin**   13. tsnahege **pheasant**
6. hbdrmuimgni **hummingbird** 14. peatreak **parakeet**
7. onol   **loon**   15. ggela   **eagle**
8. idnmcegkriob **mockingbird** 16. maiofgln **flamingo**

46

Page 47

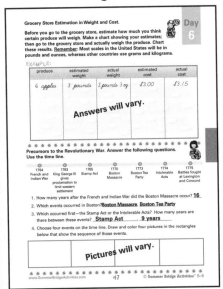

Grocery Store Estimation in Weight and Cost.

Day 6

Before you go to the grocery store, estimate how much you think certain produce will weigh. Make a chart showing your estimates; then go to the grocery store and actually weigh the produce. Chart these results. **Remember:** Most scales in the United States will be in pounds and ounces, whereas other countries use grams and kilograms.

EXAMPLE:

produce	estimated weight	actual weight	estimated cost	actual cost
6 apples	3 pounds	2 pounds 3 oz	$3.00	$3.15
		Answers will vary.		

Precursors to the Revolutionary War. Answer the following questions. Use the time line.

1754	1763	1765	1770	1773	1774	1775
French and Indian War	King George III gives proclamation to limit western settlement	Stamp Act	Boston Massacre	Boston Tea Party	Intolerable Acts	Battles fought at Lexington and Concord

1. How many years after the French and Indian War did the Boston Massacre occur? **16**

2. Which events occurred in Boston? **Boston Massacre, Boston Tea Party**

3. Which occurred first—the Stamp Act or the Intolerable Acts? How many years are there between these events? **Stamp Act 9 years**

4. Choose four events on the time line. Draw and color four pictures in the rectangles below that show the sequence of those events.

	Pictures will vary.

47

Page 48

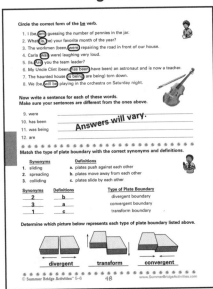

Circle the correct form of the be verb.

1. I (be, **am**) guessing the number of pennies in the jar.
2. What (**is**, be) your favorite month of the year?
3. The workmen (been, **were**) repairing the road in front of our house.
4. Carla (**was**) laughing very loud.
5. (Is, **Are**) you the team leader?
6. My Uncle Clint (been, **has been**) an astronaut and is now a teacher.
7. The haunted house (**is being**, are being) torn down.
8. We (be, **will be**) playing in the orchestra on Saturday night.

Now write a sentence for each of these words. Make sure your sentences are different from the ones above.

9. were
10. has been   _Answers will vary._
11. was being
12. are

Match the type of plate boundary with the correct synonyms and definitions.

Synonyms
1. sliding
2. spreading
3. colliding

Definitions
a. plates push against each other
b. plates move away from each other
c. plates slide by each other

Synonyms	Definitions	Type of Plate Boundary
2	b	divergent boundary
3	a	convergent boundary
1	c	transform boundary

Determine which picture below represents each type of plate boundary listed above.

divergent   transform   convergent

48

Page 49

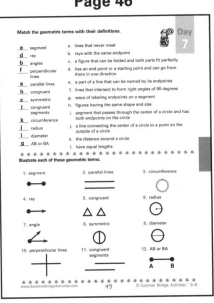

Match the geometric terms with their definitions.

Day 7

e segment   a. lines that never meet
d ray   b. rays with the same endpoint
b angles   c. a figure that can be folded and both parts fit perfectly
f perpendicular lines   d. has an end point or a starting point and can go from there in one direction
a parallel lines   e. a part of a line that can be named by its endpoints
h congruent   f. lines that intersect to form right angles of 90 degrees
c symmetric   g. ways of labeling endpoints on a segment
c congruent segments   h. figures having the same shape and size
k circumference   i. segment that passes through the center of a circle and has both endpoints on the circle
j radius   j. a line connecting the center of a circle to a point on the outside of a circle
i diameter   k. the distance around a circle
g AB or BA   l. have equal lengths

Illustrate each of these geometric terms.

1. segment   2. parallel lines   3. circumference

4. ray   5. congruent   6. radius

7. angle   8. symmetric   9. diameter

10. perpendicular lines   11. congruent segments   12. AB or BA

49

Page 50

Read this part of the Declaration of Independence and answer the questions below.

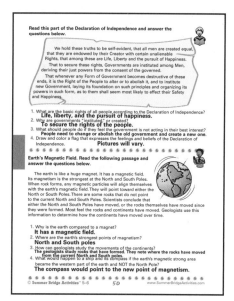

We hold these truths to be self-evident, that all men are created equal, that they are endowed by their Creator with certain unalienable Rights, that among these are Life, Liberty and the pursuit of Happiness. That to secure these rights, Governments are instituted among Men, deriving their just powers from the consent of the governed. That whenever any Form of Government becomes destructive of these ends, it is the Right of the People to alter or to abolish it, and to institute new Government, laying its foundation on such principles and organizing its powers in such form, as to them shall seem most likely to effect their Safety and Happiness.

1. What are the basic rights of all people according to the Declaration of Independence?
   Life, liberty, and the pursuit of happiness.
2. Why are governments "instituted," or created?
   To secure the rights of the people.
3. What should people do if they feel the government is not acting in their best interest?
   People need to change or abolish the old government and create a new one.
4. Draw and color a flag that expresses the feelings and beliefs of the Declaration of Independence. **Pictures will vary.**

Earth's Magnetic Field. Read the following passage and answer the questions below.

The earth is like a huge magnet. It has a magnetic field. Its magnetism is the strongest at the North and South Poles. When rock forms, any magnetic particles will align themselves with the earth's magnetic field. They will point toward either the North or South Poles. There are some rocks that do not point to the current North and South Poles. Scientists conclude that either the North and South Poles have moved, or the rocks themselves have moved since they were formed. Most feel the rocks and continents have moved. Geologists use this information to determine how the continents have moved over time.

1. Why is the earth compared to a magnet?
   It has a magnetic field.
2. Where are the earth's strongest points of magnetism?
   North and South poles
3. How can geologists study the movements of the continents?
   The geologists study rocks that have formed. They note where the rocks have moved from the current North and South poles.
4. What would happen to a ship and its compass if the earth's magnetic strong area became the western part of the earth and NOT the North Pole?
   The compass would point to the new point of magnetism.

© Summer Bridge Activities™ 5–6   50   www.SummerBridgeActivities.com

Page 51

Find the Perimeter.

Remember: To find the perimeter, you have to add the lengths of each side.

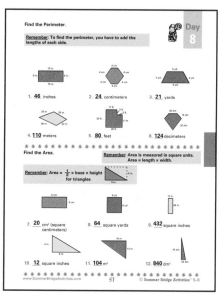

1. **46** inches
2. **24** centimeters
3. **21** yards
4. **110** meters
5. **80** feet
6. **124** decimeters

Find the Area.

Remember: Area is measured in square units. Area = length × width.

Remember: Area = ½ base × height for triangles

7. **20** cm² (square centimeters)
8. **64** square yards
9. **432** square inches
10. **12** square inches
11. **104** m²
12. **840** dm²

www.SummerBridgeActivities.com   51   © Summer Bridge Activities™ 5–6

Day 8

Page 52

Many earthquakes occur at the plate boundaries. Study the following map of earthquake epicenters and answer the questions below.

1. Color the areas with the most earthquake activity. What pattern do you see?
   Most earthquakes occur in narrow curving zones.
2. Review the map on plate boundaries on page 42. What is similar about these boundaries and earthquake activity?
   Most earthquakes occur where there are plate boundaries.
3. Explain how you came up with your answer for question 2.
   Force acts on the rocks at plate boundaries. This causes a fracture in the rocks.
4. Observe the earthquakes that occur in the interior of the plates (e.g., China, U.S., and Australia). How is the distribution of these earthquakes different from that of earthquakes along the plate boundaries?
   There are fewer and they are more spread out.

© Summer Bridge Activities™ 5–6   52   www.SummerBridgeActivities.com

Page 53

Write the rest of the number families.

Day 9

1. 78 × 42 = 3,276
   42 × 78 = 3,276
   3,276 ÷ 42 = 78
   3,276 ÷ 78 = 42

2. 39 × 56 = 2,184
   56 × 39 = 2,184
   2,184 ÷ 56 = 39
   2,184 ÷ 39 = 56

3. 95 × 37 = 3,515
   37 × 95 = 3,515
   3,515 ÷ 37 = 95
   3,515 ÷ 95 = 37

4. 49 × 76 = **3,724**
   76 × 49 = 3,724
   3,724 ÷ 76 = 49
   3,724 ÷ 49 = 76

5. 141 × 27 = **3,807**
   27 × 141 = 3,807
   3,807 ÷ 27 = 141
   3,807 ÷ 141 = 27

6. 3,762 ÷ 38 = **99**
   3,762 ÷ 99 = 38
   99 × 38 = 3,762
   38 × 99 = 3,762

7. 26,320 ÷ 47 = **560**
   26,320 ÷ 560 = 47
   560 × 47 = 26,320
   47 × 560 = 26,320

8. 48,306 ÷ 83 = **582**
   48,306 ÷ 582 = 83
   582 × 83 = 48,306
   83 × 582 = 48,306

9. 194 × 92 = **17,848**
   92 × 194 = 17,848
   17,848 ÷ 92 = 194
   17,848 ÷ 194 = 92

10. 16,019 ÷ 83 = **193**
    16,019 ÷ 193 = 83
    193 × 83 = 16,019
    83 × 193 = 16,019

11. 2,650 × 54 = **143,100**
    54 × 2,650 = 143,100
    143,100 ÷ 54 = 2,650
    143,100 ÷ 2,650 = 54

12. 876,600 ÷ 360 = **2,435**
    876,600 ÷ 2,435 = 360
    2,435 × 360 = 876,600
    360 × 2,435 = 876,600

There are a lot of ways you can take care of your respiratory system. Some ways are exercising regularly, not smoking, and not inhaling chemicals produced by products such as paint or glue. Look at some old magazines and ask your parents if you can cut out pictures of people caring for their respiratory system. If you don't have any old magazines, draw and color pictures.

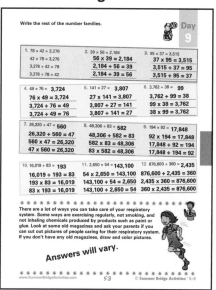

Answers will vary.

www.SummerBridgeActivities.com   53   © Summer Bridge Activities™ 5–6

Page 54

Read these paragraphs. Draw a line through the sentence or sentences that do not belong in the paragraph. Tell why.

Remember to ask yourself:
1. Does the paragraph have one main idea?
2. Do all the sentences in the paragraph tell about the main idea?
3. Is every sentence in the paragraph a complete sentence?

1. Water in the ocean never stops moving. The most well-known movements are waves. Waves are set in motion by earthquakes, winds, and the gravitational pull of the sun and moon. ~~Ocean water is also very salty.~~ On shore, we see waves caused by the wind. Their size depends on whether they come from far across the ocean or are caused by winds from nearby storms.
   It does not tell about the main idea.

2. The beaver is a furry animal with a flat, wide tail that looks like a paddle. There are more beavers in the U.S. and Canada than anywhere else. The beaver's strong front teeth are used for cutting down trees. They use the branches to build dams and homes, but they eat the bark from them too. ~~Beavers almost always swim.~~ We often call people who work hard "eager beavers."
   It is not a complete sentence.

3. Write a paragraph. Try to remember the three rules as you write.
   Answers will vary.

Earthquakes. Fill in the blanks in the paragraph with the words listed.

seismologists   seismic waves   fault   above   focus
earthquake   energy   epicenter   fracture   beneath

An **earthquake** is sudden shaking of the ground that happens when **energy** stored in rock is released. A **fault** is a break, or **fracture**, in the earth's crust. As rock breaks, stored energy moves along the fault. The hypocenter, or **focus**, is where an earthquake begins. This occurs **beneath** the earth's surface. The point on the earth's crust which is directly **above** the focus is called the **epicenter**. **Seismic waves** or shock waves, move out from the focus and cause the ground to shake. **Seismologists** study and record these shock waves and determine the size of the earthquake.

© Summer Bridge Activities™ 5–6   54   www.SummerBridgeActivities.com

Page 55

In 1617, John Napier used a method of multiplying with rods marked with numbers. Some people call it "Napier's Bones" or "lattice" multiplication. When placing the appropriate "bones" side by side, you read the product of multiplication.

Day 10

EXAMPLE: 528 × 347 = 183,216

Build your "lattice" by multiplying the digits of the factors you are multiplying. For the example, go 5 over and 3 down on the big chart to get ⅕ go 2 over and 3 down to find etc. Then, starting in the lower right corner, add along the diagonals of your lattice, carrying the remainder to the next diagonal.

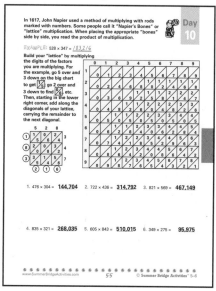

1. 476 × 304 = **144,704**
2. 722 × 436 = **314,792**
3. 821 × 569 = **467,149**
4. 835 × 321 = **268,035**
5. 605 × 843 = **510,015**
6. 349 × 275 = **95,975**

www.SummerBridgeActivities.com   55   © Summer Bridge Activities™ 5–6

Page 56

Some key words and punctuation marks signal that an author is giving a context clue. These include dashes, commas, parentheses, and phrases like which is, in other words, for instance, and etc. In these sentences write what the underlined words mean. Then write the key words or punctuation marks that helped you tell the word's meaning.

EXAMPLE: The candidate shouted through a megaphone (large funnel-shaped horn) so the crowd could hear him.
megaphone *Large funnel-shaped horn*   *parentheses*

1. I feel torpid—sluggish and lazy—in the hot summer weather.
   torpid **sluggish and lazy; dashes**
2. Paul Bunyan used an adze, which is a flat-bladed ax, to cut down the forest.
   adze **flat-bladed ax; which is**
3. The cook made ragout, a highly seasoned stew, every day for the ranch hands.
   ragout **highly seasoned stew; commas**
4. Jason mashed his patella, in other words, his kneecap.
   patella **kneecap; in other words**
5. David can play a marimba (a xylophone).
   marimba **an instrument with bars like a xylophone; parentheses**

Write your own sentences using a word many people would not know. Use context clues in each one.

6. _____ **Sentences will vary.**
7. _____

Add a prefix or a suffix to the following base words. Choose six of the words you made and write sentences with them. **Answers will vary.**

1. **dis** agree
2. **mis** placed
3. **dis** respect **ful**
4. **in** capable
5. avoid **able**
6. **ex** change
7. delay **ed**
8. **un** number **ed**
9. loyal **ty**
10. hazard **ous**
11. care **less**
12. **in** depend **ent**
13. **un** necessary
14. smart **est**
15. thought **ful**
16. marvel **ous**
17. **ad** verb
18. **im** mature
19. **un** comfort **able**
20. **im** plant
21. act **or**

© Summer Bridge Activities™ 5–6   56   www.SummerBridgeActivities.com

Page 57

Mixed Practice. Find the missing factors.

Day 11

1. 67 × **8** = 536
2. 96 × **9** = 864
3. **5** × 77 = 385
4. **11** × 84 = 924
5. 2,210 × **26** = 85
6. 5,518 × **89** = 62
7. 29 × **68** = 1,972
8. 19,347 × **877** = 18,470
9. 23,432 × **657** = 24,089
10. 32 × **200** = 6,400
11. **150** × 75 = 11,250
12. 4,905 × **15** = 327
13. 56,993 × **1,395** = 55,598
14. 4,266 × **6** = 711
15. 33 × **542** = 17,886
16. **5,529** × 34,561 = 40,090
17. 307 × **59** = 18,113
18. 741 × **83** = 61,503
19. 50,000 ÷ **40** = 1,250
20. **286** × 56 = 16,016
21. 40,572 × **322** = 126
22. 19,263 × **47,127** = 66,390
23. 73,477 × **11,172** = 62,305
24. 190,498 × **80,399** = 110,099

The Revolutionary War. Answer **T** for true or **F** for false to the following statements. If false, correct the statement so it will be true.

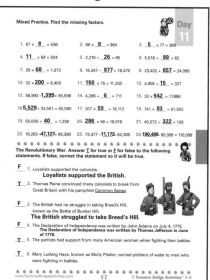

F 1. Loyalists supported the colonists.
   Loyalists supported the British.

T 2. Thomas Paine convinced many colonists to break from Great Britain with his pamphlet Common Sense.

F 3. The British had no struggle in taking Breed's Hill, known as the Battle of Bunker Hill.
   The British struggled to take Breed's Hill.

F 4. The Declaration of Independence was written by John Adams on July 4, 1775.
   The Declaration of Independence was written by Thomas Jefferson in June of 1776.

F 5. The patriots had support from many American women when fighting their battles.

T 6. Mary Ludwig Hays, known as Molly Pitcher, carried pitchers of water to men who were fighting in battles.

© Summer Bridge Activities™ 5–6   57   www.SummerBridgeActivities.com

Page 58

Irregular Verbs. Change the present form of the verb at the first of the sentence to the past form. Write the past form in the blank.

EXAMPLE:
wear   I **wore** an old coat to school.

ring   1. The telephone **rang** ten times before she answered it.
build   2. The contractor **built** a new apartment building every year.
feed   3. Aunt Dawn **fed** her cats three times a day.
choose 4. We each **chose** a friend to go with us to Disneyland.
spend   5. My brother **spent** all of his allowance on ice cream.
spin   6. The top **spun** for five minutes.
run   7. Our family **ran** in a marathon two summers ago.
eat   8. The monkey **ate** four bananas.
shake   9. I was so afraid of the dark that I **shook** when the lights went out.
hold   10. Kit **held** his breath for one minute.
bleed   11. My nose **bled** for half an hour last night.
draw   12. The class **drew** pictures showing what they did on their field trip.
ride   13. Alexander **rode** his Shetland pony in the rodeo parade last summer.
teach   14. Julie's mother **taught** us how to jump double Dutch.
fight   15. My sisters and I **fought** a lot when we were children.

Quotes.

Make a list of favorite or frequently used quotes among your family and friends. Have your family and friends help you compile your list.

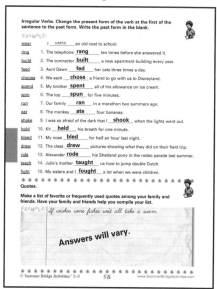

EXAMPLE: *If wishes were fishes we'd all take a swim*

Answers will vary.

© Summer Bridge Activities™ 5–6   58   www.SummerBridgeActivities.com

Day 12

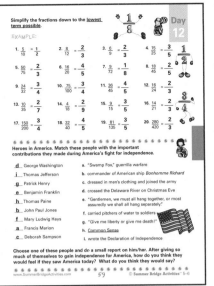

Simplify the fractions down to the lowest term possible.

EXAMPLE:

1. $\frac{5}{10} = \frac{1}{2}$
2. $\frac{8}{12} = \frac{2}{3}$
3. $\frac{6}{9} = \frac{2}{3}$
4. $\frac{15}{25} = \frac{3}{5}$
5. $\frac{50}{75} = \frac{2}{3}$
6. $\frac{16}{20} = \frac{4}{5}$
7. $\frac{9}{72} = \frac{1}{8}$
8. $\frac{18}{45} = \frac{2}{5}$
9. $\frac{24}{32} = \frac{3}{4}$
10. $\frac{75}{100} = \frac{3}{4}$
11. $\frac{36}{45} = \frac{4}{5}$
12. $\frac{16}{24} = \frac{2}{3}$
13. $\frac{10}{35} = \frac{2}{7}$
14. $\frac{4}{18} = \frac{2}{9}$
15. $\frac{9}{15} = \frac{3}{5}$
16. $\frac{14}{21} = \frac{2}{3}$
17. $\frac{150}{200} = \frac{3}{4}$
18. $\frac{32}{40} = \frac{4}{5}$
19. $\frac{81}{135} = \frac{3}{5}$
20. $\frac{280}{420} = \frac{2}{3}$

Heroes in America. Match these people with the important contributions they made during America's fight for independence.

d George Washington — a. "Swamp Fox," guerrilla warfare
i Thomas Jefferson — b. commander of American ship *Bonhomme Richard*
g Patrick Henry — c. dressed in men's clothing and joined the army
e Benjamin Franklin — d. crossed the Delaware River on Christmas Eve
h Thomas Paine — e. "Gentlemen, we must all hang together, or most assuredly we shall all hang separately."
b John Paul Jones — f. carried pitchers of water to soldiers
f Mary Ludwig Hays — g. "Give me liberty or give me death!"
a Francis Marion — h. Common Sense
c Deborah Sampson — i. wrote the Declaration of Independence

Choose one of these people and do a small report on him/her. After giving so much of themselves to gain independence for America, how do you think they would feel if they saw America today? What do you think they would say?

www.SummerBridgeActivities.com 59 © Summer Bridge Activities™ 5–6

Page 59

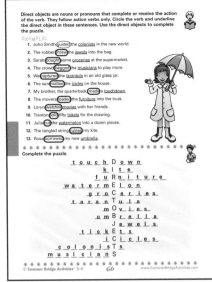

Direct objects are nouns or pronouns that complete or receive the action of the verb. They follow action verbs only. Circle the verb and underline the direct object in these sentences. Use the direct objects to complete the puzzle.

EXAMPLE:
1. John Smith (guided) the colonists in the new world.
2. The robber (threw) the jewels into the bag.
3. Sarah (bought) some groceries at the supermarket.
4. The crowd (begged) the musicians to play more.
5. We (captured) the tarantula in an old glass jar.
6. The sun (melted) the icicles on the house.
7. My brother, the quarterback, (made) a touchdown.
8. The movers (loaded) the furniture into the truck.
9. Loryn (watches) movies with her friends.
10. Trenton (sold) fifty tickets for the drawing.
11. Julia (cut) the watermelon into a dozen pieces.
12. The tangled string (ruined) my kite.
13. Rosa (borrowed) my new umbrella.

Complete the puzzle.

touchDown
kIte
fuRniture
watermElon
groCeries
taranTula
mOvies
umBrella
Jewels
tickEts
iCicles
colonisTs
musicianS

© Summer Bridge Activities™ 5–6 60 www.SummerBridgeActivities.com

Page 60

Day 13

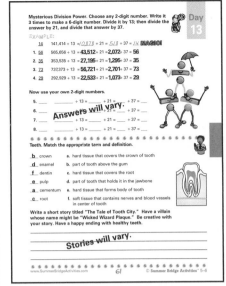

Mysterious Division Power. Choose any 2-digit number. Write it 3 times to make a 6-digit number. Divide it by 13; then divide the answer by 21, and divide that answer by 37.

EXAMPLE:
14 141,414 ÷ 13 = 10,878 ÷ 21 = 518 ÷ 37 = 14 MAGIC!
1. 56 565,656 ÷ 13 = 43,512 ÷ 21 = 2,072 ÷ 37 = 56
2. 35 353,535 ÷ 13 = 27,195 ÷ 21 = 1,295 ÷ 37 = 35
3. 73 737,373 ÷ 13 = 56,721 ÷ 21 = 2,701 ÷ 37 = 73
4. 29 292,929 ÷ 13 = 22,533 ÷ 21 = 1,073 ÷ 37 = 29

Now use your own 2-digit numbers.

5. ___ ______ ÷ 13 = ____ ÷ 21 = ___ ÷ 37 = ___
6. ___ ______ ÷ 13 = ____ ÷ 21 = ___ ÷ 37 = ___
7. ___ ______ ÷ 13 = ____ ÷ 21 = ___ ÷ 37 = ___
8. ___ ______ ÷ 13 = ____ ÷ 21 = ___ ÷ 37 = ___

Answers will vary.

Teeth. Match the appropriate term and definition.

b crown — a. hard tissue that covers the crown of tooth
d enamel — b. part of tooth above the gum
f dentin — c. hard tissue that covers the root
e pulp — d. part of tooth that holds it in the jawbone
a cementum — e. hard tissue that forms body of tooth
c root — f. soft tissue that contains nerves and blood vessels in center of tooth

Write a short story titled "The Tale of Tooth City." Have a villain whose name might be "Wicked Wizard Plaque." Be creative with your story. Have a happy ending with healthy teeth.

Stories will vary.

www.SummerBridgeActivities.com 61 © Summer Bridge Activities™ 5–6

Page 61

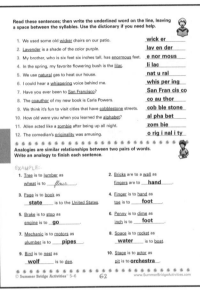

Read these sentences; then write the underlined word on the line, leaving a space between the syllables. Use the dictionary if you need help.

1. We used some old wicker chairs on our patio. — wick er
2. Lavender is a shade of the color purple. — lav en der
3. My brother, who is six feet six inches tall, has enormous feet. — e nor mous
4. In the spring, my favorite flowering bush is the lilac. — li lac
5. We use natural gas to heat our house. — nat u ral
6. I could hear a whispering voice behind me. — whis per ing
7. Have you ever been to San Francisco? — San Fran cis co
8. The coauthor of my new book is Carla Powers. — co au thor
9. We think it's fun to visit cities that have cobblestone streets. — cob ble stone
10. How old were you when you learned the alphabet? — al pha bet
11. Allen acted like a zombie after being up all night. — zom bie
12. The comedian's originality was amusing. — o rig i nal i ty

Analogies are similar relationships between two pairs of words. Write an analogy to finish each sentence.

EXAMPLE:
1. Tree is to lumber as wheat is to flour.
2. Bricks are to a wall as fingers are to hand.
3. Page is to book as state is to the United States.
4. Finger is to hand as toe is to foot.
5. Brake is to stop as engine is to go.
6. Penny is to dime as inch is to foot.
7. Mechanic is to motors as plumber is to pipes.
8. Space is to rocket as water is to boat.
9. Bird is to nest as wolf is to den.
10. Stage is to actor as pit is to orchestra.

© Summer Bridge Activities™ 5–6 62 www.SummerBridgeActivities.com

Page 62

Day 14

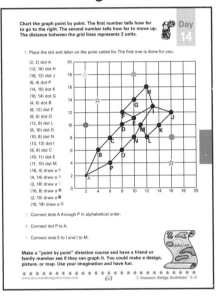

Chart the graph point by point. The first number tells how far to go to the right. The second number tells how far to move up. The distance between the grid lines represents 2 units.

1. Place the dot and letter on the point called for. The first one is done for you.

(2, 2) dot A
(12, 16) dot H
(16, 12) dot J
(6, 4) dot P
(14, 10) dot K
(10, 14) dot G
(4, 6) dot B
(8, 12) dot F
(8, 6) dot O
(12, 8) dot L
(8, 10) dot D
(10, 8) dot N
(13, 13) dot I
(6, 8) dot C
(10, 11) dot E
(11, 10) dot M
(16, 4) draw a ☆
(4, 14) draw a ☆
(2, 18) draw a ☆
(16, 8) draw a ●
(2, 10) draw a ●
(10, 18) draw a ●

2. Connect dots A through P in alphabetical order.
3. Connect dot P to A.
4. Connect dots E to I and I to M.

Make a "point by point" direction course and have a friend or family member see if they can graph it. You could make a design, picture, or map. Use your imagination and have fun.

www.SummerBridgeActivities.com 63 © Summer Bridge Activities™ 5–6

Page 63

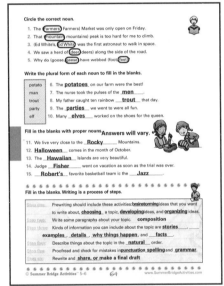

Circle the correct noun.

1. The (Farmers) Farmers) Market was only open on Friday.
2. That (mountain) mountains) peak is too hard for me to climb.
3. (Ed White's, (Ed White) was the first astronaut to walk in space.
4. We saw a herd of (deer) deers) along the side of the road.
5. Why do (goose, (geese) have webbed (foot, (feet)?

Write the plural form of each noun to fill in the blanks.

potato / man / trout / party / elf

6. The potatoes on our farm were the best!
7. The nurse took the pulses of the men.
8. My father caught ten rainbow trout that day.
9. The parties we went to were all fun.
10. Many elves worked on the shoes for the queen.

Fill in the blanks with proper nouns. Answers will vary.

11. We live very close to the Rocky Mountains.
12. Halloween comes in the month of October.
13. The Hawaiian Islands are very beautiful.
14. Judge Fisher went on vacation as soon as the trial was over.
15. Robert's favorite basketball team is the Jazz.

Fill in the blanks. Writing is a process of steps.

Step one: Prewriting should include these activities: brainstorming ideas that you want to write about, choosing a topic, developing ideas, and organizing ideas.
Step two: Write some paragraphs about your topic. composition
Step three: Kinds of information you can include about the topic are stories, examples, details, why things happen, and facts.
Step four: Describe things about the topic in the natural order.
Step five: Proofread and check for mistakes in punctuation, spelling and grammar.
Step six: Rewrite and share, or make a final draft

© Summer Bridge Activities™ 5–6 64 www.SummerBridgeActivities.com

Page 64

Day 15

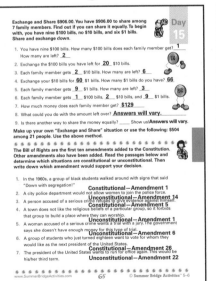

Exchange and Share $906.00. You have $906.00 to share among 7 family members. Find out if you can share it equally. To begin with, you have nine $100 bills, no $10 bills, and six $1 bills. Share and exchange down.

1. You have nine $100 bills. How many $100 bills does each family member get? 1 How many are left? 2
2. Exchange the $100 bills you have left for 20 $10 bills.
3. Each family member gets 2 $10 bills. How many are left? 6
4. Exchange your $10 bills for 60 $1 bills. How many $1 bills do you have? 66
5. Each family member gets 9 $1 bills. How many are left? 3
6. Each family member gets 1 $100 bills, 2 $10 bills, and 9 $1 bills.
7. How much money does each family member get? $129
8. What could you do with the amount left over? Answers will vary.
9. Is there another way to share the money equally? ____ Show us! Answers will vary.

Make up your own "Exchange and Share" situation or use the following: $504 among 21 people. Use the above method.

The Bill of Rights are the first ten amendments added to the Constitution. Other amendments also have been added. Read the passages below and determine which situations are constitutional or unconstitutional. Then write down which amendment would support your decision.

1. In the 1960s, a group of black students walked around with signs that said "Down with segregation!" Constitutional—Amendment 1
2. A city police department would not allow women to join the police force. Unconstitutional—Amendment 14
3. A person accused of a serious crime refuses to give evidence against himself. Constitutional—Amendment 5
4. A town does not like the religious beliefs of a particular group, so it forbids that group to build a place where they can worship. Unconstitutional—Amendment 1
5. A woman accused of a serious crime wants a trial with a jury. The government says she doesn't have enough money for this type of trial. Unconstitutional—Amendment 6
6. A group of students who just turned eighteen want to vote for whom they would like as the next president of the United States. Constitutional—Amendment 26
7. The president of the United States wants to run for office again. This would be his/her third term. Unconstitutional—Amendment 22

www.SummerBridgeActivities.com 65 © Summer Bridge Activities™ 5–6

Page 65

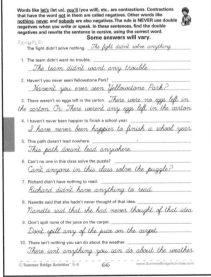

Words like let's (let us), you'll (you will), etc., are contractions. Contractions that have the word not in them are called negatives. Other words like nothing, never, and nobody are also negatives. The rule is NEVER use double negatives when you write or speak. In these sentences, find the double negatives and rewrite the sentence in cursive, using the correct word. Some answers will vary.

EXAMPLE:
The fight didn't solve nothing. *The fight didn't solve anything*

1. The team didn't want no trouble. *The team didn't want any trouble.*
2. Haven't you never seen Yellowstone Park? *Haven't you ever seen Yellowstone Park?*
3. There weren't no eggs left in the carton. *There were no eggs left in the carton. Or: There weren't any eggs left in the carton.*
4. I haven't never been happier to finish a school year. *I have never been happier to finish a school year.*
5. This path doesn't lead nowhere. *This path doesn't lead anywhere.*
6. Can't no one in this class solve the puzzle? *Can't anyone in this class solve the puzzle?*
7. Richard didn't have nothing to read. *Richard didn't have anything to read.*
8. Nanette said that she hadn't never thought of that idea. *Nanette said that she had never thought of that idea.*
9. Don't spill none of the juice on the carpet. *Don't spill any of the juice on the carpet.*
10. There isn't nothing you can do about the weather. *There isn't anything you can do about the weather.*

© Summer Bridge Activities™ 5–6 66 www.SummerBridgeActivities.com

Page 66

Day 16

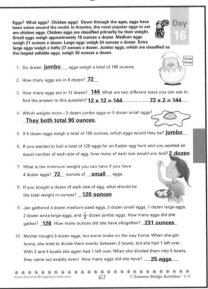

Eggs? What eggs? Chicken eggs! Down through the ages, eggs have been eaten around the world. In America, the most popular eggs to eat are chicken eggs. Chicken eggs are classified primarily by their weight. Small eggs weigh approximately 18 ounces a dozen. Medium eggs weigh 21 ounces a dozen. Large eggs weigh 24 ounces a dozen. Extra large eggs weigh a hefty 27 ounces a dozen. Jumbo eggs, which are classified as the largest sellable eggs, weigh 30 ounces a dozen.

1. Six dozen jumbo eggs weigh a total of 180 ounces.
2. How many eggs are in 6 dozen? 72
3. How many eggs are in 12 dozen? 144 What are two different ways you can use to find the answer to this question? 12 x 12 = 144, 72 x 2 = 144
4. Which weighs more—3 dozen jumbo eggs or 5 dozen small eggs? They both total 90 ounces.
5. If 5 dozen eggs weigh a total of 150 ounces, which eggs would they be? jumbo
6. If you wanted to boil a total of 120 eggs for an Easter egg hunt and you wanted an equal number of each size of egg, how many of each size would you boil? 2 dozen
7. What is the minimum weight you can have if you have 4 dozen eggs? 72 ounces of small eggs.
8. If you bought a dozen of each size of egg, what should be the total weight in ounces? 120 ounces
9. Jan gathered 4 dozen medium-sized eggs, 3 dozen small eggs, 1 dozen large eggs, 2 dozen extra-large eggs, and $\frac{1}{2}$ dozen jumbo eggs. How many eggs did she gather? 126 How many ounces did she have altogether? 231 ounces
10. Mother bought 3 dozen eggs, but some broke on the way home. When she got home, she tried to divide them evenly between 2 bowls, but she had 1 left over. With 3 and 4 bowls she again had 1 left over. When she divided them into 5 bowls, they came out exactly even! How many eggs did she have? 25 eggs

www.SummerBridgeActivities.com 67 © Summer Bridge Activities™ 5–6

Page 67

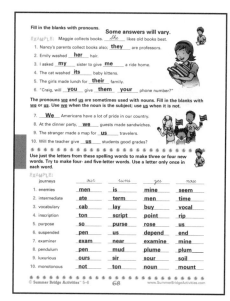

Page 68

Fill in the blanks with pronouns. **Some answers will vary.**

EXAMPLE: Maggie collects books. _she_ likes old books best.

1. Nancy's parents collect books also; _they_ are professors.
2. Emily washed _her_ hair.
3. I asked _my_ sister to give _me_ a ride home.
4. The cat washed _its_ baby kittens.
5. The girls made lunch for _their_ family.
6. "Craig, will _you_ give _them_ _your_ phone number?"

The pronouns we and us are sometimes used with nouns. Fill in the blanks with we or us. Use we when the noun is the subject; use us when it is not.

7. _We_ Americans have a lot of pride in our country.
8. At the dinner party, _we_ guests made sandwiches.
9. The stranger made a map for _us_ travelers.
10. Will the teacher give _us_ students good grades?

Use just the letters from these spelling words to make three or four new words. Try to make four- and five-letter words. Use a letter only once in each word.

EXAMPLE:
journeys

	our	runs	yes	nose
1. enemies	men	is	mine	seem
2. intermediate	ate	term	men	time
3. vocabulary	cab	lay	buy	vocal
4. inscription	ton	script	point	rip
5. purpose	so	purse	rose	us
6. suspended	pen	us	depend	end
7. examiner	exam	near	examine	mine
8. pendulum	pen	mud	plume	plum
9. luxurious	ours	sir	sour	soil
10. monotonous	not	ton	noun	mount

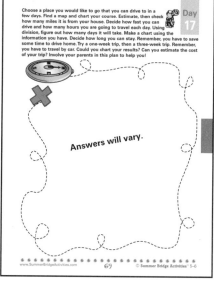

Page 69

Choose a place you would like to go that you can drive to in a few days. Find a map and chart your course. Estimate, then check how many miles it is from your house. Decide how fast you can drive and how many hours you are going to travel each day. Using division, figure out how many days it will take. Make a chart using the information you have. Decide how long you can stay. Remember, you have to save some time to drive home. Try a one-week trip, then a three-week trip. Remember, you have to travel by car. Could you chart your results? Can you estimate the cost of your trip? Involve your parents in this plan to help you!

Answers will vary.

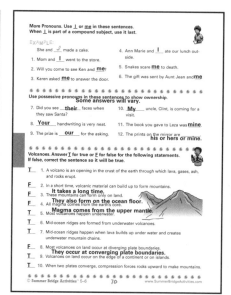

Page 70

Day 17

More Pronouns. Use I or me in these sentences. When I is part of a compound subject, use it last.

EXAMPLE:
She and _I_ made a cake.

1. Mom and _I_ went to the store.
2. Will you come to see Ken and _me_?
3. Karen asked _me_ to answer the door.
4. Ann Marie and _I_ ate our lunch outside.
5. Snakes scare _me_ to death.
6. The gift was sent from Aunt Jean and _me_.

Use possessive pronouns in these sentences to show ownership. **Some answers will vary.**

7. Did you see _their_ faces when they saw Santa?
8. _Your_ handwriting is very neat.
9. The prize is _our_ for the asking.
10. _My_ uncle, Clint, is coming for a visit.
11. The book you gave to Leza was _mine_.
12. The prints on the mirror are _his or hers or mine._

Volcanoes. Answer T for true or F for false for the following statements. If false, correct the sentence so it will be true.

_T_ 1. A volcano is an opening in the crust of the earth through which lava, gases, ash, and rocks erupt.
_F_ 2. In a short time, volcanic material can build up to form mountains. **It takes a long time,**
_F_ 3. These mountains can form only on land. **They also form on the ocean floor.**
_F_ 4. All magma comes from the earth's core. **Magma comes from the upper mantle.**
_T_ 5. Most volcanoes happen underwater.
_T_ 6. Mid-ocean ridges are formed from underwater volcanoes.
_T_ 7. Mid-ocean ridges happen when lava builds up under water and creates underwater mountain chains.
_F_ 8. Most volcanoes on land occur at diverging plate boundaries. **They occur at converging plate boundaries.**
_T_ 9. Volcanoes on land occur on the edge of a continent or on islands.
_T_ 10. When two plates converge, compression forces rocks upward to make mountains.

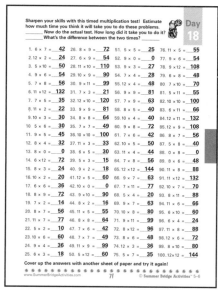

Page 71

Day 18

Sharpen your skills with this timed multiplication test! Estimate how much time you think it will take you to do these problems. ____ Now do the actual test. How long did it take you to do it? ____ What's the difference between the two times? ____

1. 6 × 7 = **42**
2. 12 × 2 = **24**
3. 5 × 10 = **50**
4. 9 × 6 = **54**
5. 7 × 8 = **56**
6. 11 × 12 = **132**
7. 7 × 5 = **35**
8. 11 × 2 = **22**
9. 10 × 3 = **30**
10. 5 × 6 = **30**
11. 9 × 5 = **45**
12. 8 × 4 = **32**
13. 8 × 0 = **0**
14. 6 × 12 = **72**
15. 8 × 3 = **24**
16. 10 × 2 = **20**
17. 6 × 6 = **36**
18. 8 × 9 = **72**
19. 7 × 2 = **14**
20. 8 × 7 = **56**
21. 11 × 7 = **77**
22. 5 × 2 = **10**
23. 10 × 6 = **60**
24. 9 × 4 = **36**
25. 6 × 3 = **18**
26. 8 × 9 = **72**
27. 6 × 9 = **54**
28. 11 × 10 = **110**
29. 10 × 9 = **90**
30. 9 × 11 = **99**
31. 3 × 7 = **21**
32. 12 × 10 = **120**
33. 9 × 9 = **81**
34. 8 × 8 = **64**
35. 7 × 7 = **49**
36. 10 × 10 = **100**
37. 11 × 3 = **33**
38. 7 × 5 = **35**
39. 5 × 3 = **15**
40. 9 × 2 = **18**
41. 12 × 5 = **60**
42. 10 × 0 = **0**
43. 9 × 10 = **90**
44. 8 × 2 = **16**
45. 11 × 5 = **55**
46. 8 × 8 = **64**
47. 7 × 6 = **42**
48. 7 × 7 = **49**
49. 11 × 9 = **99**
50. 5 × 12 = **60**
51. 5 × 5 = **25**
52. 7 × 8 = **56**
53. 9 × 3 = **27**
54. 7 × 4 = **28**
55. 12 × 4 = **48**
56. 9 × 9 = **81**
57. 9 × 7 = **63**
58. 5 × 8 = **40**
59. 10 × 4 = **40**
60. 9 × 8 = **72**
61. 7 × 6 = **42**
62. 10 × 5 = **50**
63. 11 × 4 = **44**
64. 7 × 8 = **56**
65. 12 × 6 = **72**
66. 9 × 7 = **63**
67. 11 × 7 = **77**
68. 5 × 4 = **20**
69. 7 × 9 = **63**
70. 10 × 8 = **80**
71. 9 × 11 = **99**
72. 8 × 12 = **96**
73. 8 × 6 = **48**
74. 7 × 5 = **35**
75. 3 × 7 = **21**
76. 11 × 5 = **55**
77. 7 × 8 = **56**
78. 9 × 12 = **108**
79. 6 × 8 = **48**
80. 7 × 10 = **70**
81. 5 × 11 = **55**
82. 10 × 10 = **100**
83. 6 × 11 = **66**
84. 12 × 9 = **108**
85. 8 × 7 = **56**
86. 8 × 7 = **56**
87. 5 × 8 = **40**
88. 9 × 11 = **99**
89. 7 × 3 = **21**
90. 11 × 8 = **88**
91. 11 × 12 = **132**
92. 10 × 7 = **70**
93. 8 × 11 = **88**
94. 11 × 6 = **66**
95. 6 × 10 = **60**
96. 6 × 4 = **24**
97. 8 × 8 = **64**
98. 12 × 6 = **72**
99. 10 × 8 = **80**
100. 12 × 12 = **144**

Cover up the answers with another sheet of paper and try it again!

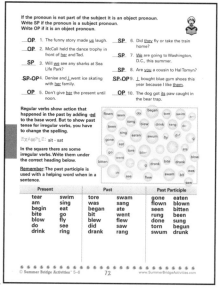

Page 72

If the pronoun is not part of the subject it is an object pronoun. Write SP if the pronoun is a subject pronoun. Write OP if it is an object pronoun.

_OP_ 1. The funny story made _us_ laugh.
_OP_ 2. McCall held the dance trophy in front of _her_ and Ted.
_SP_ 3. Will _we_ see any sharks at Sea Life Park?
_SP-OP_ 4. Denise and _I_ went ice skating with _her_ family.
_OP_ 5. Don't give _her_ the present until noon.
_SP_ 6. Did _they_ fly or take the train home?
_SP_ 7. _We_ are going to Washington, D.C., this summer.
_SP_ 8. Are _you_ a cousin to Hal Tomyn?
_SP-OP_ 9. _I_ bought blue gym shoes this year because I like _them_.
_OP_ 10. The dog got _its_ paw caught in the bear trap.

Regular verbs show action that happened in the past by adding -ed to the base word. But to show past tense for irregular verbs, you have to change the spelling.

EXAMPLE: sit - sat

In the square there are some irregular verbs. Write them under the correct heading below.

Remember: The past participle is used with a helping word when in a sentence.

Present		Past		Past Participle	
tear	swim	tore	swam	gone	eaten
am	sing	was	sang	flown	blown
begin	eat	began	ate	seen	bitten
bite	go	bit	went	rung	been
blow	fly	blew	flew	done	sung
do	see	did	saw	torn	begun
drink	ring	drank	rang	swum	drunk

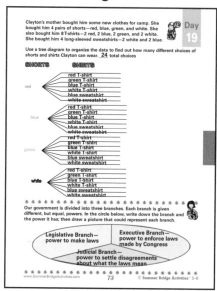

Page 73

Day 19

Clayton's mother bought him some new clothes for camp. She bought him 4 pairs of shorts—red, blue, green, and white. She also bought him 8 T-shirts—2 red, 2 blue, 2 green, and 2 white. She bought him 4 long-sleeved sweatshirts—2 white and 2 blue.

Use a tree diagram to organize the data to find out how many different choices of shorts and shirts Clayton can wear. **24** total choices

SHORTS   SHIRTS

red
- red T-shirt
- green T-shirt
- white T-shirt
- blue sweatshirt
- white sweatshirt

blue
- red T-shirt
- green T-shirt
- blue T-shirt
- white T-shirt
- blue sweatshirt
- white sweatshirt

green
- red T-shirt
- green T-shirt
- white T-shirt
- blue sweatshirt
- white sweatshirt

white
- red T-shirt
- green T-shirt
- blue T-shirt
- white T-shirt
- blue sweatshirt
- white sweatshirt

Our government is divided into three branches. Each branch is given different, but equal, powers. In the circle below, write down the branch and the power it has; then draw a picture that could represent each branch.

Legislative Branch— power to make laws
Executive Branch— power to enforce laws made by Congress
Judicial Branch— power to settle disagreements about what the laws mean

---

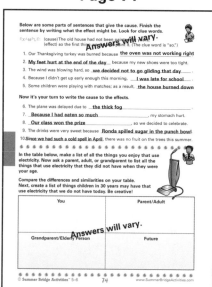

Page 74

Below are some parts of sentences that give the cause. Finish the sentence by writing what the effect might be. Look for clue words.

EXAMPLE: (cause) The old house had not been painted in years. **Answers will vary.** (effect) so the first thing we did was paint it. (The clue word is "so.")

1. Our Thanksgiving turkey was burned because **the oven was not working right**
2. My feet hurt at the end of the day, because my new shoes were too tight.
3. The wind was blowing hard, so **we decided not to go gliding that day**
4. Because I didn't get up early enough this morning, **I was late for school**
5. Some children were playing with matches; as a result, **the house burned down**

Now it's your turn to write the cause to the effects.

6. The plane was delayed due to **the thick fog**
7. **Because I had eaten so much** my stomach hurt.
8. **Our class won the prize** so we decided to celebrate.
9. The drinks were very sweet because **Ronda spilled sugar in the punch bowl**
10. Since we had such a cold spell in April, there was no fruit on the trees this summer.

In the table below, make a list of all the things you enjoy that use electricity. Now ask a parent, adult, or grandparent to list all the things that use electricity that they did not have when they were your age.

Compare the differences and similarities on your table. Next, create a list of things children in 30 years may have that use electricity that we do not have today. Be creative!

You	Parent/Adult
	Answers will vary.
Grandparent/Elderly Person	Future

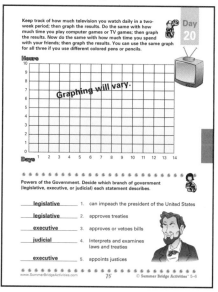

Page 75

Day 20

Keep track of how much television you watch daily in a two-week period; then graph the results. Do the same with how much time you play computer games or TV games; then graph the results. Now do the same with how much time you spend with your friends; then graph the results. You can use the same graph for all three if you use different colored pens or pencils.

Hours

Graphing will vary.

Days

Powers of the Government. Decide which branch of government (legislative, executive, or judicial) each statement describes.

legislative 1. can impeach the president of the United States
legislative 2. approves treaties
executive 3. approves or vetoes bills
judicial 4. Interprets and examines laws and treaties
executive 5. appoints justices

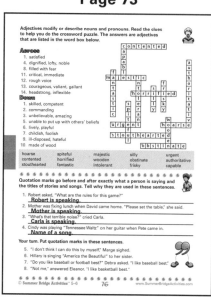

Page 76

Adjectives modify or describe nouns and pronouns. Read the clues to help you do the crossword puzzle. The answers are adjectives that are listed in the word box below.

Across
1. satisfied
3. dignified, lofty, noble
8. filled with fear
11. critical, immediate
12. rough voice
13. courageous, valiant, gallant
14. headstrong, inflexible

Down
1. skilled, competent
2. commanding
4. unbelievable, amazing
5. unable to put up with others' beliefs
6. lively, playful
7. childish, foolish
9. ill-disposed, hateful
10. made of wood

hoarse	spiteful	majestic	silly	urgent
contented	horrified	wooden	obstinate	authoritative
stouthearted	fantastic	intolerant	frisky	capable

Crossword answers: contented, authoritative, majestic, horrified, urgent, hoarse, stouthearted

Quotation marks go before and after exactly what a person is saying and the titles of stories and songs. Tell why they are used in these sentences.

1. Robert asked, "What are the rules for this game?" **Robert is speaking.**
2. Mother was fixing lunch when David came home. "Please set the table," she said. **Mother is speaking.**
3. "What's that terrible noise?" cried Carla. **Carla is speaking.**
4. Cindy was playing "Tennessee Waltz" on her guitar when Pete came in. **Name of a song.**

Your turn. Put quotation marks in these sentences.

5. I don't think I can do this by myself, Marge sighed.
6. Hillary is singing America the Beautiful to her sister.
7. Do you like baseball or football best? Debra asked. I like baseball best.
8. Not me, answered Eleanor. I like basketball best.

Section 3

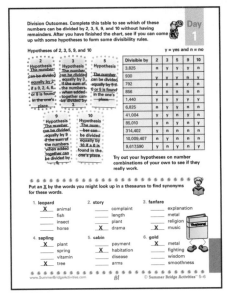

Page 81

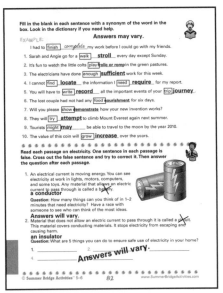

Page 82

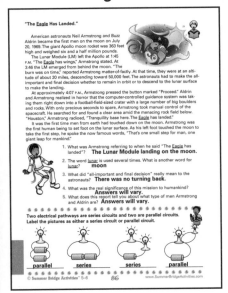

Page 83

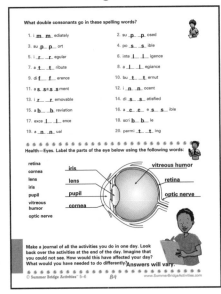

Page 84

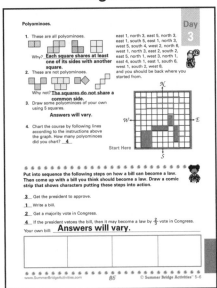

Page 85

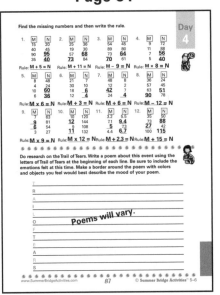

Page 86

Page 87

Page 88

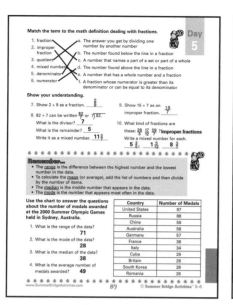
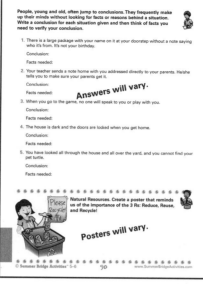
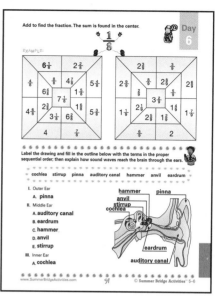

Page 89

Match the term to the math definition dealing with fractions.

1. fraction — a. The answer you get by dividing one number by another number
2. improper fraction — b. The number found below the line in a fraction
3. quotient — c. A number that names a part of a set or part of a whole
4. mixed number — d. The number found above the line in a fraction
5. denominator — e. A number that has a whole number and a fraction
6. numerator — f. A fraction whose numerator is greater than its denominator or can be equal to its denominator

Show your understanding.

7. Show 2 ÷ 9 as a fraction. $\frac{2}{9}$
8. 82 ÷ 7 can be written $\frac{82}{7}$ or 7)82.
   What is the divisor? 7
   What is the remainder? 5
   Write it as a mixed number. $11\frac{5}{7}$
9. Show 15 ÷ 7 as an improper fraction. $\frac{15}{7}$
10. What kind of fractions are these: $\frac{28}{17}$ $\frac{52}{42}$ $\frac{97}{7}$? **improper fractions**
   Write a mixed number for each.
   $5\frac{3}{4}$ $1\frac{1}{2}$ $8\frac{2}{3}$

Remember...
- The **range** is the difference between the highest number and the lowest number in the data.
- To calculate the **mean** (or average), add the list of numbers and then divide by the number of items.
- The **median** is the middle number that appears in the data.
- The **mode** is the number that appears most often in the data.

Use the chart to answer the questions about the number of medals awarded at the 2000 Summer Olympic Games held in Sydney, Australia.

Country	Number of Medals
United States	97
Russia	88
China	59
Australia	58
Germany	57
France	38
Italy	34
Cuba	29
Britain	28
South Korea	28
Romania	26

1. What is the range of the data? 71
2. What is the mode of the data? 28
3. What is the median of the data? 38
4. What is the average number of medals awarded? 49

Page 90

People, young and old, often jump to conclusions. They frequently make up their minds without looking for facts or reasons behind a situation. Write a conclusion for each situation given and then think of facts you need to verify your conclusion.

1. There is a large package with your name in it at your doorstep without a note saying who it's from. It's not your birthday.
   Conclusion:
   Facts needed:

2. Your teacher sends a note home with you addressed directly to your parents. He/she tells you to make sure your parents get it.
   Conclusion:
   Facts needed:

3. When you go to the game, no one will speak to you or play with you.
   Conclusion:
   Facts needed:

4. The house is dark and the doors are locked when you get home.
   Conclusion:
   Facts needed:

5. You have looked all through the house and all over the yard, and you cannot find your pet turtle.
   Conclusion:
   Facts needed:

Answers will vary.

Natural Resources. Create a poster that reminds us of the importance of the 3 Rs: Reduce, Reuse, and Recycle!

Posters will vary.

Page 91

Add to find the fraction. The sum is found in the center. $\frac{1}{8}$

EXAMPLE:

Label the drawing and fill in the outline below with the terms in the proper sequential order; then explain how sound waves reach the brain through the ears.

cochlea stirrup pinna auditory canal hammer anvil eardrum

I. Outer Ear
 A. pinna
II. Middle Ear
 A. auditory canal
 B. eardrum
 C. hammer
 D. anvil
 E. stirrup
III. Inner Ear
 A. cochlea

Page 92

Underline the adverb in each sentence. At the end of the sentence, write the word it modifies.

1. The cat's broken leg hurts badly. **hurts**
2. The train moved rapidly down the tracks. **moved**
3. That chorus sang well. **sang**
4. Our three bulldogs waited eagerly for their walk. **waited**
5. The monkeys chattered noisily in the trees. **chattered**

Fill in the blanks with adverbs. **Answers will vary.**

6. The child sat **carefully** on the stairs.
7. Delicate white snowflakes were falling **gently** to the ground.
8. Kirk spoke **quietly** to his father on the phone.
9. April drove her new car **proudly** through the middle of town.
10. The old windmill worked **perfectly** after he oiled it.

Categories. Find the word that does not belong in the category. Draw a line through it and write a sentence using the word you drew a line through to tell why it doesn't belong.

EXAMPLE:
street - road - railroad - freeway - highway *Cars do not travel on a railroad.*

1. software - mouse - depth - program - disk
   Depth has nothing to do with computers.
2. dawn - daytime - twilight - sunrise - hyphen
   A hyphen is a punctuation mark.
3. spaghetti - meatballs - menu - rhubarb - lasagna
   I do not want to eat the menu.
4. cyclone - generator - tornado - hurricane - monsoon
   A generator is not related to the weather.
5. mythology - petrology - geology - biology - zoology
   Mythology is the study of myths.

Page 93

Watching for Zeros with Decimals. Remember the extra zeros when necessary.

1. 41.5 × 0.17 = 7.055
2. 1.09 × 0.68 = 0.7412
3. 3.05 × 85.2 = 259.860
4. 0.003 × 3.9 = 0.0117
5. 7.4 × 0.07 = 0.518
6. 0.09 × 2.3 = 0.207
7. 0.035 × 0.02 = 0.00070
8. 0.005 × 55 = 0.275
9. 27.5 × 0.91 = 25.025
10. 60 × 0.005 = 0.300
11. 0.92 × 12.5 = 11.500
12. 1.08 × 2.03 = 2.1924

Read the following scenarios. After reading each sentence, determine whether proper first aid procedures are being followed. Make a smiley face if they were done correctly. Make an X if they were not done correctly.

Scenario 1: Dallin fell off his bike and saw a big bruise forming on his leg.
☺ He immediately put ice on it.
☺ Next, he used compression by applying pressure with a cloth on the bruise.
☺ Dallin then elevated his leg.

Scenario 2: While Jana and Adam were playing, a dog bit Adam.
X Jana chased the dog for two blocks trying to capture it.
☺ When she came back, Jana called her mom to help Adam.
X Jana thought they should put butter on the wound.
☺ Jana's mom washed the bite with soap and water.
☺ They took Adam to the doctor's office.
☺ Jana's mom called animal control.

Scenario 3: Linda felt dizzy and fainted.
☺ Stephen quickly caught her from falling.
☺ He gently put her to the floor and raised her feet.
☺ He turned Linda's face to the side in case she vomited.
X Mac suggested they slap or throw water on Linda to wake her up.
☺ Stephen said, "No, let's get an adult to help us."

*As a child, an important thing to remember with first aid is to get emergency help. Make a card of phone numbers you can call in an emergency. Put it by your phone.

Page 94

Answer T for true or F for false to the following statements about a discussion group. Tell why you think the false statements are false.

T 1. You talk with others about an idea.
F 2. The leader of the group should do most of the talking.
F 3. The leader's only job is to keep things moving.
T 4. It is important to listen to what is being said.
T 5. Everyone should have a turn to talk.
F 6. The people in the group should not ask questions.
T 7. Disagreeing is okay in a discussion group.
T 8. One of the leader's duties is to keep order.
T 9. All participants should be polite to one another.
T 10. The discussion leader should sum up what has been decided or discussed at the end of the session.

Pollution is a problem that affects all people on the earth. Match the definition with the correct word. Put a smiley face to the column if this term helps with pollution problems. Put a sad face if it does not help our environment. If it is a sad face, come up with an idea about how we can improve in this area!

1. a tanker runs aground and leaks oil
2. energy generated from falling water
3. food for gardens from leaves and clippings
4. exhaust from cars and pollution from factories create a layer of pollution; heat rays from sun cannot go back into the atmosphere
5. energy generated from the inside of the earth
6. poisonous materials like paint thinner
7. saving
8. smoke and exhaust that mix with water vapor
9. waste taken to a dump that is eventually covered with earth

4 greenhouse effect
6 hazardous waste
8 acid rain
3 compost
7 conservation
5 geothermal energy
2 hydroelectric energy
9 landfill
1 oil spill

	Smiley or Sad	Idea
		Answers will vary

Page 95

Finding the Circumference.

showing the radius of a circle | showing the diameter of a circle | circumference is the distance around a circle

Remember: To find the circumference of a circle, you must multiply the diameter by 3.14. With this information, complete the missing data in the table below.

	Radius of the Circle	Diameter of the Circle	Circumference of the Circle
1.	12 mm	24 mm	75.36 mm
2.	11 inches	22 inches	69.08 inches
3.	9 cm	18 cm	56.52 cm
4.	10 meters	20 meters	62.80 meters
5.	13 yards	26 yards	81.64 yards
6.	24 feet	48 feet	150.72 feet
7.	21 inches	42 inches	131.88 inches
8.	17 cm	34 cm	106.76 cm
9.	45 mm	90 mm	282.60 mm
10.	50 inches	100 inches	314 inches

Women's Rights. Because of women such as Lucy Stone, Susan B. Anthony, Lucretia Mott, Elizabeth Cady Stanton, and Sarah and Angelina Grimke, women have many rights today that they didn't have in earlier times. Research one of these women and write of the trials she had to go through because of what she believed.

Answers will vary.

Page 96

Adjectives tell how many, what kind, or which one about the nouns or pronouns they modify. Fill in the blanks with these kinds of adjectives. Use two adjectives telling how many, two telling what kind, and one telling which one. At the end of the sentence, tell what kind you used.

1. **(any number)** cars got stuck in the traffic jam. how many
2. **That or This** adventure was the most exciting I've ever had. which one
3. The **furry or fluffy** teddy bear cost twenty-five dollars. what kind
4. There were **fewer or more** camels than lions at the zoo. how many
5. The **(any color)** lizard that came after us was huge. what kind

Articles: Special Adjectives (a, an, the). Circle the correct word.

6. Was that (a, **an**, the) alligator or (**a**, an) crocodile we saw back there?
7. The student gave her teacher (**a**, an) crisp, red apple.
8. (A, **An**, the) excited child was playing with (**a**, an) fluffy kitten.
9. After (a, an) rainstorm (a, an, **the**) sun glistens on (a, an, **the**) puddles.
10. If March comes in like (a, an, **the**) lion, it should go out like (a, an, **the**) lamb.

Take a word from list A and a word from list B to make compound words. Write the compound word in the middle. A word in list B could be the first word in the compound.

1. spacecraft
2. loudspeaker
3. shipwreck
4. vineyard
5. anchorwoman
6. wristwatch
7. typewriter
8. newsprint
9. silverware
10. bloodhound
11. lifeguard
12. clipboard
13. peppermint
14. turtleneck
15. frostbite

A: craft, ware, loud, blood, ship, guard, vine, clip, anchor, mint, watch, turtle, type, frost, print

B: speaker, wreck, silver, writer, wrist, board, yard, pepper, neck, woman, space, bite, hound, life, news

Page 97

Multiplying Fractions Pictures.

Question: How do you picture what $\frac{1}{2}$ of $\frac{1}{3}$ is?

Picture $\frac{1}{2}$ of a box as $\frac{1}{2}$ of 1. Now picture what $\frac{1}{2}$ of $\frac{1}{3}$ is. So $\frac{1}{2}$ of $\frac{1}{3}$ = $\frac{1}{6}$, or 1 ÷ 2 ÷ 3 = $\frac{1}{6}$.

With the above information, illustrate and answer the following multiplication problems. Reduce to the simplest terms.
Remember: When you multiply fractions, the product gets smaller.

1. $\frac{1}{2} \times \frac{1}{3} = \frac{1}{6}$
2. $\frac{1}{4} \times \frac{1}{2} = \frac{1}{8}$
3. $\frac{2}{3} \times \frac{1}{2} = \frac{1}{3}$
4. $\frac{1}{6} \times \frac{1}{2} = \frac{1}{12}$
5. $\frac{2}{5} \times \frac{4}{5} = \frac{8}{25}$
6. $\frac{2}{3} \times \frac{2}{3} = \frac{4}{9}$
7. $\frac{1}{4} \times \frac{1}{2} = \frac{1}{8}$
8.
9.
10. $\frac{3}{4} \times \frac{2}{3} = \frac{1}{2}$

Early Inventions in America. Match the inventor with his invention. Then sketch an invention of your own and explain in detail how it would work and why it would be a good idea.

d. Eli Whitney — a. telegraph
c. Elias Howe — b. phonograph
g. Levi Strauss — c. sewing machine
f. Cyrus McCormick — d. cotton gin
a. Samuel F. B. Morse — e. telephone
b. Thomas Edison — f. reaper
e. Alexander G. Bell — g. blue jeans

Answers will vary.

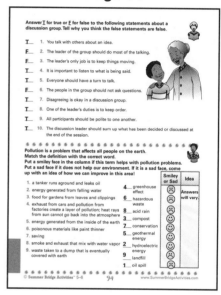
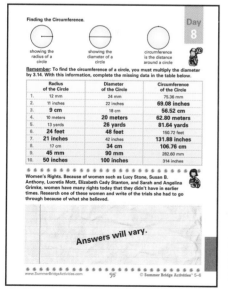
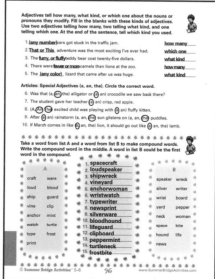
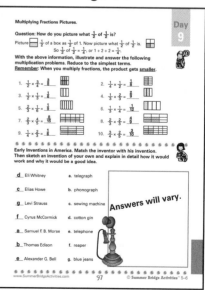

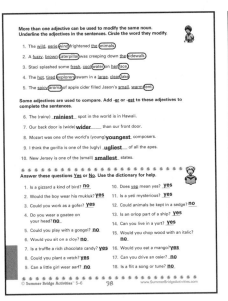

Page 98

More than one adjective can be used to modify the same noun. Underline the adjectives in the sentences. Circle the word they modify.

1. The wild, eerie wind frightened the animals.
2. A fuzzy, brown caterpillar was creeping down the sidewalk.
3. Staci splashed some fresh, cool water on her face.
4. The hot, tired explorers swam in a large, clean lake.
5. The spicy aroma of apple cider filled Jason's small, warm tent.

Some adjectives are used to compare. Add -er or -est to these adjectives to complete the sentences.

6. The (rainy) __rainiest__ spot in the world is in Hawaii.
7. Our back door is (wide) __wider__ than our front door.
8. Mozart was one of the world's (young) __youngest__ composers.
9. I think the gorilla is one of the (ugly) __ugliest__ of all the apes.
10. New Jersey is one of the (small) __smallest__ states.

Answer these questions Yes or No. Use the dictionary for help.

1. Is a gizzard a kind of bird? __no__
2. Would the boy wear his mukluk? __yes__
3. Could you work as a gofer? __yes__
4. Do you wear a goatee on your head? __no__
5. Could you play with a googol? __no__
6. Would you sit on a cloy? __no__
7. Is a truffle a rich chocolate candy? __yes__
8. Could you plant a vetch? __yes__
9. Can a little girl wear aarf? __no__
10. Does vep mean yes? __yes__
11. Is a yeti mysterious? __yes__
12. Could animals be kept in a sedge? __no__
13. Is an orlop part of a ship? __yes__
14. Can you live in a yurt? __yes__
15. Would you chop wood with an italic? __no__
16. Would you eat a mango? __yes__
17. Can you drive an osier? __no__
18. Is a flit a song or tune? __no__

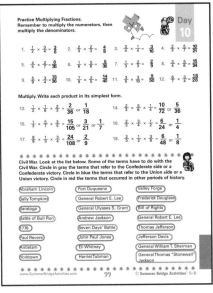

Page 99

Day 10

Practice Multiplying Fractions. Remember to multiply the numerators, then multiply the denominators.

1. $\frac{1}{2} \times \frac{2}{3} = \frac{2}{6}$ 2. $\frac{2}{5} \times \frac{2}{3} = \frac{4}{15}$ 3. $\frac{3}{4} \times \frac{1}{4} = \frac{3}{16}$ 4. $\frac{2}{3} \times \frac{5}{7} = \frac{10}{21}$
5. $\frac{4}{5} \times \frac{2}{7} = \frac{8}{35}$ 6. $\frac{1}{6} \times \frac{1}{5} = \frac{1}{30}$ 7. $\frac{3}{7} \times \frac{1}{2} = \frac{3}{14}$ 8. $\frac{2}{9} \times \frac{3}{4} = \frac{6}{36}$
9. $\frac{5}{9} \times \frac{4}{4} = \frac{5}{36}$ 10. $\frac{2}{7} \times \frac{2}{6} = \frac{4}{42}$ 11. $\frac{3}{5} \times \frac{3}{10} = \frac{9}{50}$ 12. $\frac{4}{7} \times \frac{3}{4} = \frac{12}{28}$

Multiply. Write each product in its simplest form.

13. $\frac{1}{2} \times \frac{1}{6} \times \frac{2}{3} = \frac{2}{36}$ or $\frac{1}{18}$ 14. $\frac{2}{3} \times \frac{5}{6} \times \frac{1}{2} = \frac{10}{72}$ or $\frac{5}{36}$
15. $\frac{1}{3} \times \frac{5}{7} \times \frac{3}{5} = \frac{15}{105}$ or $\frac{3}{21}$ 16. $\frac{2}{3} \times \frac{3}{4} \times \frac{1}{2} = \frac{6}{24}$ or $\frac{1}{4}$
17. $\frac{8}{9} \times \frac{1}{3} \times \frac{3}{4} = \frac{24}{108}$ or $\frac{2}{9}$ 18. $\frac{2}{3} \times \frac{1}{2} \times \frac{3}{8} = \frac{6}{48}$ or $\frac{1}{8}$

Civil War. Look at the list below. Some of the terms have to do with the Civil War. Circle in gray the terms that refer to the Confederate side or a Confederate victory. Circle in blue the terms that refer to the Union side or a Union victory. Circle in red the terms that occurred in other periods of history.

Abraham Lincoln, Sally Tompkins, Saratoga, Battle of Bull Run, 1776, Paul Revere, Antietam, Yorktown, Fort Duquesne, General Robert E. Lee, General Ulysses S. Grant, Andrew Jackson, Seven Days' Battle, John Paul Jones, Eli Whitney, Harriet Tubman, Valley Forge, Frederick Douglass, Bill of Rights, General Robert E. Lee, Thomas Jefferson, Jefferson Davis, General William T. Sherman, General Thomas "Stonewall" Jackson

---

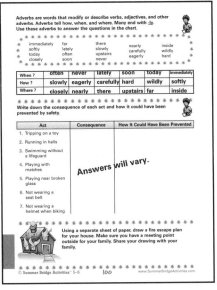

Page 100

Adverbs are words that modify or describe verbs, adjectives, and other adverbs. Adverbs tell how, when, and where. Many end with -ly. Use these adverbs to answer the questions in the chart.

immediately, softly, today, closely, far, lately, often, soon, there, slowly, upstairs, never, nearly, carefully, eagerly, inside, wildly, hard

	When?				
When?	often	never	lately	soon	today	immediately
How?	slowly	eagerly	carefully	hard	wildly	softly
Where?	closely	nearly	there	upstairs	far	inside

Write down the consequence of each act and how it could have been prevented by safety.

Act	Consequence	How It Could Have Been Prevented
1. Tripping on a toy		
2. Running in halls		
3. Swimming without a lifeguard		
4. Playing with matches	Answers will vary.	
5. Playing near broken glass		
6. Not wearing a seat belt		
7. Not wearing a helmet when biking		

Using a separate sheet of paper, draw a fire escape plan for your house. Make sure you have a meeting point outside for your family. Share your drawing with your family.

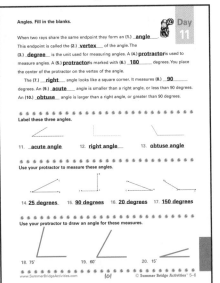

Page 101

Day 11

Angles. Fill in the blanks.

When two rays share the same endpoint they form an (1.) __angle__. This endpoint is called the (2.) __vertex__ of the angle. The (3.) __degree__ is the unit used for measuring angles. A (4.) __protractor__ is used to measure angles. A (5.) __protractor__ is marked with (6.) __180__ degrees. You place the center of the protractor on the vertex of the angle.

The (7.) __right__ angle looks like a square corner. It measures (8.) __90__ degrees. An (9.) __acute__ angle is smaller than a right angle, or less than 90 degrees. An (10.) __obtuse__ angle is larger than a right angle, or greater than 90 degrees.

Label these three angles.

11. __acute angle__ 12. __right angle__ 13. __obtuse angle__

Use your protractor to measure these angles.

14. __25 degrees__ 15. __90 degrees__ 16. __20 degrees__ 17. __150 degrees__

Use your protractor to draw an angle for these measures.

18. 75° 19. 60° 20. 15°

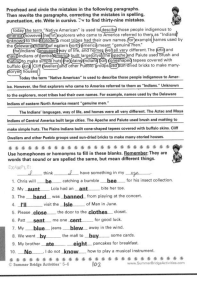

Page 102

Proofread and circle the mistakes in the following paragraphs. Then rewrite the paragraphs, correcting the mistakes in spelling, punctuation, etc. Write in cursive. There are thirty-nine mistakes.

today the term "Native American" is used to describe those people indigenous to america, however the first explorers who came to America referred to them as "Indians" unknown to the exploders, most tribes had their own names. for example names used by the delaware indians of eastern north america meant "genuine men." the indians' language, way of life, and homes wer all very different. The aztec and maya indians of central america built large citys. The apache and Paiute used brush and matting to make simple huts. the plains indians built coneshaped tepees covered with buffalo skin. Cliff Dwellers and other Pueblo groups used sun-dried bricks to make many-storyed houses.

Today the term "Native American" is used to describe those people indigenous to America. However, the first explorers who came to America referred to them as "Indians." Unknown to the explorers, most tribes had their own names. For example, names used by the Delaware Indians of eastern North America meant "genuine men."

The Indians' languages, way of life, and homes were all very different. The Aztec and Maya Indians of Central America built large cities. The Apache and Paiute used brush and matting to make simple huts. The Plains Indians built cone-shaped tepees covered with buffalo skins. Cliff Dwellers and other Pueblo groups used sun-dried bricks to make many-storied houses.

Use homophones or homonyms to fill in these blanks. Remember: They are words that sound or are spelled the same, but mean different things.

EXAMPLE: I __think__ I have something in my eye.

1. Chris will __be__ catching a bumble __bee__ for his insect collection.
2. My __aunt__ Lola had an __ant__ bite her toe.
3. The __band__ was __banned__ from playing at the concert.
4. __I'll__ visit the __Isle__ of Man in June.
5. Please __close__ the door to the __clothes__ closet.
6. Patt __sent__ me one __cent__ for good luck.
7. My __blue__ jeans __blew__ away in the wind.
8. We went __by__ the mall to __buy__ some cards.
9. My brother __ate__ __eight__ pancakes for breakfast.
10. __No__, I do not __know__ how to play a musical instrument.

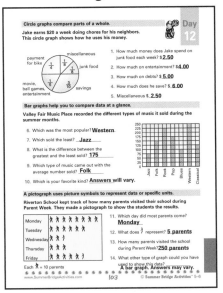

Page 103

Day 12

Circle graphs compare parts of a whole.

Jake earns $20 a week doing chores for his neighbors. This circle graph shows how he uses his money.

payment for bike $\frac{1}{4}$, miscellaneous $\frac{1}{8}$, junk food $\frac{1}{8}$, savings $\frac{3}{10}$, movie, ball games, entertainment

1. How much money does Jake spend on junk food each week? __$2.50__
2. How much on entertainment? __$4.00__
3. How much on debts? __$5.00__
4. How much does he save? __$6.00__
5. Miscellaneous $__2.50__

Bar graphs help you to compare data at a glance.

Valley Fair Music Place recorded the different types of music it sold during the summer months.

6. Which was the most popular? __Western__
7. Which sold the least? __Jazz__
8. What is the difference between the greatest and the least sold? __175__
9. Which type of music came out with the average number sold? __Folk__
10. Which is your favorite kind? __Answers will vary.__

A pictograph uses picture symbols to represent data or specific units.

Riverton School kept track of how many parents visited their school during Parent Week. They made a pictograph to show the students the results.

Monday	🚶🚶🚶🚶🚶
Tuesday	🚶🚶
Wednesday	🚶🚶🚶
Thursday	🚶🚶🚶
Friday	🚶🚶

Each 🚶 = 10 parents

11. Which day did most parents come? __Monday__
12. What does 🚶 represent? __5 parents__
13. How many parents visited the school during Parent Week? __250 parents__
14. What other type of graph could you have used to show this data? __A bar graph. Answers may vary.__

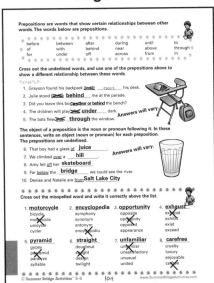

Page 104

Prepositions are words that show certain relationships between other words. The words below are prepositions.

before, between, after, during, until, to, of, with, behind, near, above, through, for, under, off, across, from, in

Cross out the underlined words, and use one of the prepositions above to show a different relationship between these words.

EXAMPLE:
1. Grayson found his backpack ~~under~~ near his desk.
2. Julie stood ~~by~~ behind me at the parade.
3. Did you leave this book ~~near~~ or ~~behind~~ the bench?
4. The children will play ~~after~~ under dark.
5. The bats flew ~~out~~ through the window.

Answers will vary.

The object of a preposition is the noun or pronoun following it. In these sentences, write an object (noun or pronoun) for each preposition. The prepositions are underlined.

6. That boy had a glass of __juice__.
7. We climbed over a __hill__.
8. Amy fell off her __skateboard__.
9. Far below the __bridge__ we could see the river.
10. Denise and Natalie are from __Salt Lake City__.

Answers will vary.

Cross out the misspelled word and write it correctly above the list.

1. __motorcycle__: bicycle, ~~motrcicle~~, unicycle, cycler
2. __encyclopedia__: symphony, synonym, antonym, ~~encyclopdiu~~
3. __opportunity__: opposite, ~~oppotunity~~, opposed, appearance
4. __exhaust__: ~~exhost~~, exhibit, exist, exceed
5. __pyramid__: gypsy, ~~peramid~~, paralyze, syllable
6. __straight__: doughnut, ~~sright~~, design, twilight
7. __unfamiliar__: ~~unfimiliar~~, unsatisfactory, unusual, united
8. __carefree__: cruelty, luxury, enjoyable, ~~carfee~~

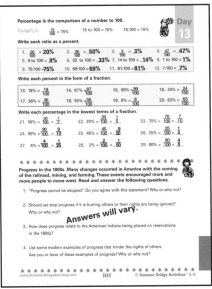

Page 105

Day 13

Percentage is the comparison of a number to 100.

EXAMPLE: $\frac{15}{100} = 15\%$ 15 to 100 = 15%   15:100 = 15%

Write each ratio as a percent.

1. $\frac{20}{100} = $ __20%__ 2. $\frac{50}{100} = $ __50%__ 3. $\frac{3}{100} = $ __3%__ 4. $\frac{47}{100} = $ __47%__
5. 9 to 100 = __9%__ 6. 33 to 100 = __33%__ 7. 14 to 100 = __14%__ 8. 1 to 100 = __1%__
9. 75:100 = __69%__ 10. 69:100 = __69%__ 11. 81:100 = __81%__ 12. 7:100 = __7%__

Write each percent in the form of a fraction.

13. 19% = $\frac{19}{100}$ 14. 87% = $\frac{87}{100}$ 15. 99% = $\frac{99}{100}$ 16. 24% = $\frac{24}{100}$
17. 36% = $\frac{36}{100}$ 18. 55% = $\frac{55}{100}$ 19. 8% = $\frac{8}{100}$ 20. 63% = $\frac{63}{100}$

Write each percentage in the lowest terms of a fraction.

21. 50% = $\frac{50}{100} = \frac{1}{2}$ 22. 20% = $\frac{20}{100} = \frac{1}{5}$ 23. 70% = $\frac{70}{100} = \frac{7}{10}$
24. 90% = $\frac{90}{100} = \frac{9}{10}$ 25. 45% = $\frac{45}{100} = \frac{9}{20}$ 26. 25% = $\frac{25}{100} = \frac{1}{4}$
27. 4% = $\frac{4}{100} = \frac{1}{25}$ 28. 2% = $\frac{2}{100} = \frac{1}{50}$ 29. 80% = $\frac{80}{100} = \frac{4}{5}$

Progress in the 1800s. Many changes occurred in America with the coming of the railroad, mining, and farming. These events encouraged more and more people to move west. Read and answer the following questions.

1. "Progress cannot be stopped." Do you agree with this statement? Why or why not?
2. Should we stop progress if it is hurting others or their rights are being ignored? Why or why not?
3. How does progress relate to the American Indians being placed on reservations in the 1800s?
4. List some modern examples of progress that hinder the rights of others. Are you in favor of these examples of progress? Why or why not?

Answers will vary.

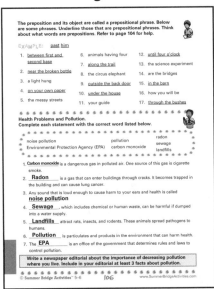

Page 106

The preposition and its object are called a prepositional phrase. Below are some phrases. Underline those that are prepositional phrases. Think about what words are prepositions. Refer to page 104 for help.

EXAMPLE: past him

1. between first and second base
2. near the broken bottle
3. a light hung
4. on your own paper
5. the messy streets
6. animals having four
7. along the trail
8. the circus elephant
9. outside the back door
10. under the house
11. your guide
12. until four o'clock
13. the science experiment
14. are the bridges
15. in the barn
16. how you will be
17. through the bushes

Health Problems and Pollution. Complete each statement with the correct word listed below.

noise pollution, pollution, Environmental Protection Agency (EPA), carbon monoxide, radon, sewage, landfills

1. __Carbon monoxide__ is a dangerous gas in polluted air. One source of this gas is cigarette smoke.
2. __Radon__ is a gas that can enter buildings through cracks. It becomes trapped in the building and can cause lung cancer.
3. Any sound that is loud enough to cause harm to your ears and health is called __noise pollution__.
4. __Sewage__, which includes chemical or human waste, can be harmful if dumped into a water supply.
5. __Landfills__ attract rats, insects, and rodents. These animals spread pathogens to humans.
6. __Pollution__ is particulates and products in the environment that can harm health.
7. The __EPA__ is an office of the government that determines rules and laws to control pollution.

Write a newspaper editorial about the importance of decreasing pollution where you live. Include in your editorial at least 3 facts about pollution.

Page 107

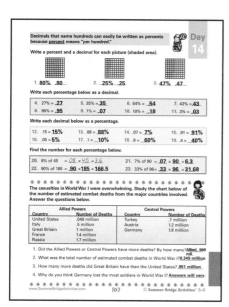

Decimals that name hundreds can easily be written as percents because **percent** means "per hundred."

Write a percent and a decimal for each picture (shaded area).

1. **80%** . **.80**
2. **25%** . **.25**
3. **47%** . **.47**

Write each percentage below as a decimal.

4. 27% = **.27**
5. 35% = **.35**
6. 54% = **.54**
7. 43% = **.43**
8. 95% = **.95**
9. 7% = **.07**
10. 18% = **.18**
11. 3% = **.03**

Write each decimal below as a percentage.

12. .15 = **15%**
13. .88 = **88%**
14. .07 = **7%**
15. .91 = **91%**
16. .05 = **5%**
17. .1 = **10%**
18. .6 = **60%**
19. .4 = **40%**

Find the number for each percentage below.

20. 8% of 45 = **.08** × **45** = **3.6**
21. 7% of 90 = **.07** × **90** = **6.3**
22. 90% of 185 = **.90** × **185** = **166.5**
23. 33% of 96 = **.33** × **96** = **31.68**

The casualties in World War I were overwhelming. Study the chart below of the number of estimated combat deaths from the major countries involved. Answer the questions below.

Allied Powers		Central Powers	
Country	Number of Deaths	Country	Number of Deaths
United States	.049 million	Turkey	.7 million
Italy	.5 million	Austria	1.2 million
Great Britain	1 million	Germany	1.8 million
France	1.4 million		
Russia	1.7 million		

1. Did the Allied Powers or Central Powers have more deaths? By how many? **Allied, .949 mil.**
2. What was the total number of estimated combat deaths in World War I? **8.349 million**
3. How many more deaths did Great Britain have than the United States? **.951 million**
4. Why do you think Germany lost the most soldiers in World War I? **Answers will vary.**

107 © Summer Bridge Activities™ 5–6

Page 108

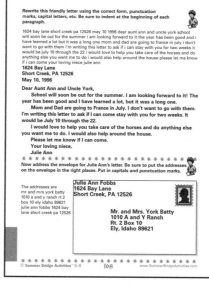

Rewrite this friendly letter using the correct form, punctuation marks, capital letters, etc. Be sure to indent at the beginning of each paragraph.

1624 bay lane short creek pa 12526 may 10 1996 dear aunt ann and uncle york school will soon be out for the summer i am looking forward to it the year has been good and i have learned a lot but it was a long one mom and dad are going to france in july i don't want to go with them i'm writing this letter to ask if i can stay with you for two weeks it would be july 10 through the 22 i would love to help you take care of the horses and do anything else you want me to do i would also help around the house please let me know if i can come your loving niece julie ann

1624 Bay Lane
Short Creek, PA 12526
May 10, 1996

Dear Aunt Ann and Uncle York,

    School will soon be out for the summer. I am looking forward to it! The year has been good and I have learned a lot, but it was a long one.

    Mom and Dad are going to France in July. I don't want to go with them. I'm writing this letter to ask if I can come stay with you for two weeks. It would be July 10 through the 22.

    I would love to help you take care of the horses and do anything else you want me to do. I would also help around the house.

    Please let me know if I can come.

    Your loving niece,
    Julie Ann

Now address the envelope for Julie Ann's letter. Be sure to put the addresses on the envelope in the right places. Put in capitals and punctuation marks.

The addresses are mr and mrs york batty 1010 a and y ranch rt 2 box 10 ely idaho 89621 julie ann fobbs 1624 bay lane short creek pa 12526

Julie Ann Fobbs
1624 Bay Lane
Short Creek, PA 12526

Mr. and Mrs. York Batty
1010 A and Y Ranch
Rt. 2 Box 10
Ely, Idaho 89621

© Summer Bridge Activities™ 5–6   108   www.SummerBridgeActivities.com

---

Page 109

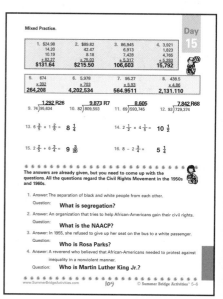

Mixed Practice.

1. $24.98	2. $89.82	3. 86,945	4. 3,921
14.20	42.47	6,913	1,823
10.19	8.18	7,428	4,765
+ 82.27	+ 75.03	+ 5,317	+ 5,283
$131.64	$215.50	106,603	15,792

5. 674	6. 5,978	7. 95.27	8. 438.5
× 392	× 703	× 5.93	× 4.86
264,208	4,202,534	564.9511	2,131.110

9. 74)95,634   **1,292 R26**
10. 82)809,593   **9,873 R7**
11. 69)593,745   **8,605**
12. 93)729,374   **7,842 R68**

13. $6\frac{3}{8} \times 1\frac{2}{8} = $ **8 ¼**
14. $2\frac{1}{2} \times 4\frac{1}{5} = $ **10 ½**
15. $2\frac{4}{5} + 6\frac{3}{4} = $ **9 ⅗**
16. $8 - 2\frac{3}{4} = $ **5 ¼**

The answers are already given, but you need to come up with the questions. All the questions regard the Civil Rights Movement in the 1950s and 1960s.

1. Answer: The separation of black and white people from each other.
Question: **What is segregation?**

2. Answer: An organization that tries to help African-Americans gain their civil rights.
Question: **What is the NAACP?**

3. Answer: In 1955, she refused to give up her seat on the bus to a white passenger.
Question: **Who is Rosa Parks?**

4. Answer: A reverend who believed that African-Americans needed to protest against inequality in a nonviolent manner.
Question: **Who is Martin Luther King Jr.?**

www.SummerBridgeActivities.com   109   © Summer Bridge Activities™ 5–6

Page 110

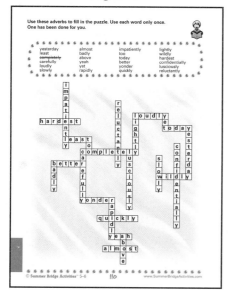

Use these adverbs to fill in the puzzle. Use each word only once. One has been done for you.

yesterday, least, completely, carefully, loudly, slowly, almost, badly, above, yeah, yet, rapidly, impatiently, too, today, better, yonder, quickly, lightly, wildly, hardest, confidentially, lusciously, reluctantly

© Summer Bridge Activities™ 5–6   110   www.SummerBridgeActivities.com

---

Better Bodies   Better Behavior

Up until now, **Summer Bridge Activities**™ has been all about your mind...

But the other parts of you—who you are, how you act, and how you feel—are important too. These pages are all about helping build a better you this summer.

Keeping your body strong and healthy helps you live better, learn better, and feel better. To keep your body healthy, you need to do things like eat right, get enough sleep, and exercise. The Physical Fitness pages of Building Better Bodies will teach you about good eating habits and the importance of proper exercise. You can even train for a Presidential Fitness Award over the summer.

The Character pages are all about building a better you on the inside. They've got fun activities for you and your family to do together. The activities will help you develop important values and habits you'll need as you grow up.

After a summer of Building Better Bodies and Behavior and **Summer Bridge Activities**™, there may be a whole new you ready for school in the fall!

For Parents: Introduction to Character Education

Character education is simply giving your child clear messages about the values you and your family consider important. Many studies have shown that a basic core of values is universal. You will find certain values reflected in the laws of every country and incorporated in the teachings of religious, ethical, and other belief systems throughout the world.

The character activities included here are designed to span the entire summer. Each week your child will be introduced to a new value, with a quote and two activities that illustrate it. Research has shown that character education is most effective when parents reinforce the values in their child's daily routine; therefore, we encourage parents to be involved as their child completes the lessons.

Here are some suggestions on how to maximize these lessons.
- Read through the lesson yourself. Then set aside a block of time for you and your child to discuss the value.
- Plan a block of time to work on the suggested activities.
- Discuss the meaning of the quote with your child. Ask, "What do you think the quote means?" Have your child ask other members of the family the same question. If possible, include grandparents, aunts, uncles, and cousins.
- Use the quote as often as you can during the week. You'll be pleasantly surprised to learn that both you and your child will have it memorized by the end of the week.
- For extra motivation, you can set a reward for completing each week's activities.
- Point out to your child other people who are actively displaying a value. Example: "See how John is helping Mrs. Olsen by raking her leaves."
- Be sure to praise your child each time he or she practices a value: "Mary, it was very courteous of you to wait until I finished speaking."
- Find time in your day to talk about values. Turn off the radio in the car and chat with your children; take a walk in the evening as a family; read a story about the weekly value at bedtime; or give a back rub while you talk about what makes your child happy or sad.
- Finally, model the values you want your child to acquire. Remember, children will do as you do, not as you say.

How I Measure Up!

You will be filling in this page twice—once now and once at the end of the summer to see how you have grown. Have an adult help you measure yourself to fill in the blanks below.

around the neck ____|____

smile ____|____

neck to belly button ____|____

around the wrist ____|____

neck to belly button ____|____

around the wrist ____|____

around the waist ____|____

elbow to wrist ____|____

shoulder to elbow ____|____

length of longest finger ____|____

around the knee ____|____

waist to ankle ____|____

around the ankle ____|____

foot length ____|____

around the neck ____|____

smile ____|____

neck to belly button ____|____

around the wrist ____|____

around the waist ____|____

elbow to wrist ____|____

shoulder to elbow ____|____

length of longest finger ____|____

around the knee ____|____

waist to ankle ____|____

around the ankle ____|____

foot length ____|____

Nutrition

The food you eat helps your body grow. It gives you energy to work and play. Some foods give you protein or fats. Other foods provide vitamins, minerals, or carbohydrates. These are all things your body needs. Eating a variety of good foods each day will help you stay healthy. How much and what foods you need depends on many things, including whether you're a girl or boy, how active you are, and how old you are. To figure out the right amount of food for you, go to http://www.mypyramid.gov/mypyramid/index.aspx and use the Pyramid Plan Calculator. In the meantime, here are some general guidelines.

Your body needs nutrients from each food group every day.

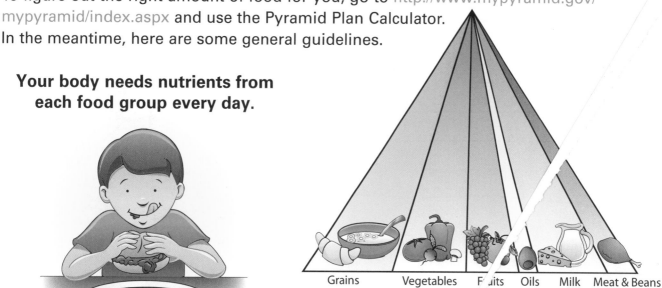

Grains	Vegetables	Fruits	Oils	Milk	Meat & Beans
4 to 5 ounce equivalents each day (an ounce might be a slice of bread, a packet of oatmeal, or a bowl of cereal)	1 1/2 cups each day	1 to 1 1/2 cups each day		1 to 2 cups of milk (or other calcium-rich food) each day	3 to 5 ounce equivalents each day

What foods did you eat today?

Which food group did you eat the most foods from today?

From which food group did you eat the least?

Which meal included the most food groups?

Meal Planning

Plan out three balanced meals for one day. Arrange your meals so that by the end of the day, you will have had all the recommended amounts of food from each food group listed on the food pyramid.

Breakfast

Lunch

Dinner

Meal Tracker

Use these charts to record the amount of food you eat from each food group for one or two weeks. Have another family member keep track, too, and compare.

	Grains	Milk	Meat & Beans	Fruits	Vegetables	Oils/ Sweets
Monday						
Tuesday						
Wednesday						
Thursday						
Friday						
Saturday						
Sunday						

	Grains	Milk	Meat & Beans	Fruits	Vegetables	Oils/ Sweets
Monday						
Tuesday						
Wednesday						
Thursday						
Friday						
Saturday						
Sunday						

	Grains	Milk	Meat & Beans	Fruits	Vegetables	Oils/ Sweets
Monday						
Tuesday						
Wednesday						
Thursday						
Friday						
Saturday						
Sunday						

	Grains	Milk	Meat & Beans	Fruits	Vegetables	Oils/ Sweets
Monday						
Tuesday						
Wednesday						
Thursday						
Friday						
Saturday						
Sunday						

Get Moving!

Did you know that getting no exercise can be almost as bad for you as smoking? So get moving this summer!

Summer is the perfect time to get out and get in shape. Your fitness program should include three parts:

• Get 30 minutes of aerobic exercise per day, three to five days a week.

• Exercise your muscles to improve strength and flexibility.

• Make it FUN! Do things that you like to do. Include your friends and family.

Couch Potato Quiz

If the time you spend on activities 4 and 5 adds up to more than you spend on 1–3, you could be headed for a spud's life!

1. Name three things you do each day that get you moving.

2. Name three things you do a few times a week that are good exercise.

3. How many hours do you spend each week playing outside or exercising?

4. How much TV do you watch each day?

5. How much time do you spend playing computer or video games?

You can find information on fitness at www.fitness.gov or www.kidshealth.org

Activity Pyramid

The Activity Pyramid works like the Food Pyramid. You can use the Activity Pyramid to help plan your summer exercise program. Fill in the blanks below.

List 1 thing that isn't good exercise that you could do less of this summer.

1._____

List 3 fun activities you enjoy that get you moving and are good exercise.

1._____
2._____
3._____

List 3 exercises you could do to build strength and flexibility this summer.

1._____
2._____
3._____

Cut Down On

TV time
video or computer games
sitting for more than
30 minutes at a time

List 3 activities you would like to do for aerobic exercise this summer.

1._____
2._____
3._____

2–3 Times a Week

Work & Play
bowling
swinging
fishing
jump rope
yard work

Strength & Stretching
dancing
martial arts
gymnastics
push-ups/pull-ups

List 2 sports you would like to participate in this summer.

1._____
2._____

3–5 Times a Week
at least 30 minutes

Aerobic Exercise
walking   skating
running   bicycling
               swimming

Sports/Recreation
soccer   relay races
basketball   tennis
volleyball   baseball

Every Day

walk
play outside
take the stairs
bathe your pet

help with chores:
sweeping
washing dishes
picking up
clothes and toys

Adapted from the President's Council on Fitness and Sports

List 5 everyday things you can do to get moving more often.

1._____
2._____
3._____
4._____
5._____

Fitness Fundamentals

Basic physical fitness includes several things:

Cardiovascular Endurance. Your cardiovascular system includes your heart and blood vessels. You need a strong heart to pump your blood which delivers oxygen and nutrients to your body.

Muscular Strength. This is how strong your muscles are.

Muscular Endurance. Endurance has to do with how long you can use your muscles before they get tired.

Flexibility. This is your ability to move your joints and to use your muscles through their full range of motion.

Body Composition. Your body is made up of lean mass and fat mass.

Lean mass includes the water, muscles, tissues, and organs in your body.

Fat mass includes the fat your body stores for energy. Exercise helps you burn body fat and maintain good body composition.

The goal of a summer fitness program is to improve in all the areas of physical fitness.

You build cardiovascular endurance through **aerobic** exercise. For **aerobic** exercise, you need to work large muscle groups at a steady pace. This increases your heart rate and breathing. You can jog, walk, hike, swim, dance, do aerobics, ride a bike, go rowing, climb stairs, rollerblade, play golf, backpack…

You should get at least 30 minutes of aerobic exercise per day, three to five days a week.

You build muscular strength and endurance with exercises that work your muscles, like sit-ups, push-ups, pull-ups, and weight lifting.

You can increase flexibility through stretching exercises. These are good for warm-ups, too.

Find these fitness words.

Word Bank

aerobic	exercise	fat
muscular	flexible	blood
endurance	strength	oxygen
heart rate	joint	hiking

```
u a e y i d t y a g d x p o b
o l s h s t r e n g t h l r c
e w l o o o z v s d m i h d t
g t z w s j o i n t m n k a o
s q a c h i p s a d e t f f m
k c q r x i q f l e x i b l e
e e j o t v k w t e u r g e g
i e s e d r v i n t n f k x o
k e l i d c a d n n e g e j w
u z e d c y u e i g g x i c i
j c i b o r e a h h y w v s i
a m r a a c e m x x x y d i g
f p v n p n d x u s o x e f k
p o c b l o o d e g z a x m c
l e m u s c u l a r m k g i s
```

Your Summer Fitness Program

Start your summer fitness program by choosing at least one aerobic activity from your Activity Pyramid. You can choose more than one for variety.

_____   _____   _____

Do this activity three to five times each week. Keep it up for at least 30 minutes each time.
(Exercise hard enough to increase your heart rate and your breathing. Don't exercise so hard that you get dizzy or can't catch your breath.)

Use this chart to plan when you will exercise, or use it as a record when you exercise.

DATE	ACTIVITY	TIME

DATE	ACTIVITY	TIME

Plan a reward for meeting your exercise goals for two weeks.
(You can make copies of this chart to track your fitness all summer long.)

Start Slow!

Remember to start out slow. Exercise is about getting stronger. It's not about being superman—or superwoman—right off the bat.

Are You Up to the Challenge?

The Presidential Physical Fitness Award Program was designed to help kids get into shape and have fun. To earn the award, you take five fitness tests. These are usually given by teachers at school, but you can train for them this summer. Make a chart to track your progress. Keep working all summer to see if you can improve your score.

 **Remember: Start Slow!**

1. Curl-ups. Lie on the floor with your knees bent and your feet about 12 inches from your buttocks. Cross your arms over your chest. Raise your trunk up and touch your elbows to your thighs. Do as many as you can in one minute.

2. Shuttle Run. Draw a starting line. Put two blocks 30 feet away. Run the 30 feet, pick up a block, and bring it back to the starting line. Then run and bring back the second block. Record your fastest time.

3. V-sit Reach. Sit on the floor with your legs straight and your feet 8 to 12 inches apart. Put a ruler between your feet, pointing past your toes. Have a partner hold your legs straight, and keep your toes pointed up. Link your thumbs together and reach forward, palms down, as far as you can along the ruler.

4. One-Mile Walk/Run. On a track or some safe area, run one mile. You can walk as often as you need to. Finish as fast as possible. (Ages six to seven may want to run a quarter mile; ages eight to nine, half a mile.)

5. Pull-ups. Grip a bar with an overhand grip (the backs of your hands toward your face). Have someone lift you up if you need help. Hang with your arms and legs straight. Pull your body up until your chin is over the bar; then let yourself back down. Do as many as you can.

Respect

Respect is showing good manners toward all people, not just those you know or who are like you. Respect is treating everyone, no matter what religion, race, or culture, male or female, rich or poor, in a way that you would want to be treated. The easiest way to do this is to decide to **never** take part in activities and to **never** use words that make fun of people because they are different from you or your friends.

It's not necessary for eagles to be crows. What I am, I am.
~ Sitting Bull

Word Search

Find these words that also mean *respect*.

Word Bank

honor
idolize
admire
worship
recognize
appreciate
venerate
prize

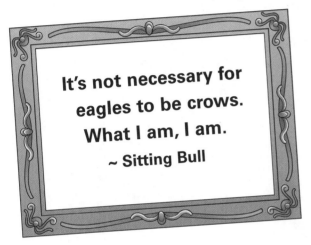

```
m c e t a r e n e v
w j t a h p s e p t
e c a d n n t z i w
z v i m w u k i h r
i e c i h b h n s o
l z e r v b j g r n
o i r e k a u o o o
d r p g m e e c w h
i p p b g c h e r j
q f a b f g u r r z
```

Activity

This week go to the library and check out *The Well: David's Story* by Mildred Taylor (1995). The story is set in Mississippi in the early 1900s and tells about David's family, who shares their well with both black and white neighbors. Be sure to read this book with your parents.

Gratitude

Gratitude is when you thank people for the good things they have given you or done for you. Thinking about people and events in your life that make you feel grateful (thankful) will help you become a happier person.

There are over 465 different ways of saying thank you. Here are a few:

Danke   **Toda**   **Merci**   **Gracias**   **Nandri**

Spasibo   **Arigato**   **Gadda ge**   **Paldies**   **Hvala**

Make a list of ten things you are grateful for.

1. _____
2. _____
3. _____
4. _____
5. _____

6. _____
7. _____
8. _____
9. _____
10. _____

A Recipe for Saying Thanks

1. Make a colorful card.
2. On the inside, write a thank-you note to someone who has done something nice for you.
3. Address an envelope to that person.
4. Pick out a cool stamp.
5. Drop your note in the nearest mailbox.

Saying thank you creates love.

~ Daphne Rose Kingma

Manners

If you were the only person in the world, you wouldn't have to have **good manners** or be **courteous**. However, there are over six billion people on our planet, and good manners help us all get along with each other.

Children with good manners are usually well liked by other children and are certainly liked by adults. Here are some simple rules for good manners:

- When you ask for something, say, "Please."
- When someone gives you something, say, "Thank you."
- When someone says, "Thank you," say, "You're welcome."
- If you walk in front of someone or bump into a person, say, "Excuse me."
- When someone else is talking, wait before speaking.
- Share and take turns.

No kindness, no matter how small, is ever wasted. ~ Aesop's Fables

Find these words or phrases that deal with *courtesy*.

Word Bank
etiquette
thank you
welcome
excuse me
please
share
turns
patience
polite
manners

```
m u o y k n a h t
e m o c l e w e e
e s a e l p x f c
a m q u f c x r n
e t t e u q i t e
s r g s n r u t i
s r e n n a m g t
v m p o l i t e a
e i e r a h s h p
```

I've Got Manners

Make a colorful poster to display on your bedroom door or on the refrigerator. List five ways you are going to practice your manners. Be creative and decorate with watercolors, poster paints, pictures cut from magazines, clip art, or geometric shapes.

Instead of making a poster, you could make a mobile to hang from your ceiling that shows five different manners to practice.

Consequences

A **consequence** is what happens after you choose to do something. Some choices lead to good consequences. Other choices lead to bad consequences. An example of this would be choosing whether to eat an apple or a bag of potato chips. The potato chips might seem like a more tasty snack, but eating an apple is better for your body. Or, you may not like to do your homework, but if you choose not to, you won't do well in school, and you may not be able to go out with your friends.

It's hard to look into the future and see how a choice will influence what happens today, tomorrow, or years from now. But whenever we choose to do something, there are consequences that go with our choice. That's why it is important to *think before you choose.*

Remember: The easiest choice does not always lead to the best consequence.

> We choose to go to the moon not because it's easy, but because it's hard.
> ~ John F. Kennedy

Activity

Get a copy of *The Tale of Peter Rabbit* by Beatrix Potter. This simple story is full of choices that lead to bad consequences. Write down three choices Peter made and the consequences that occurred. Who made a good choice, and what was the consequence?

Find these words that also mean *consequence.*

Word Bank		
result	outcome	fallout
payoff	effect	reaction
product	aftermath	upshot

```
b e h p j c p o j q
i t h a e l r w r v
z u t y f r o s t v
g o a o f e d t o m
r l m f e a u r h j
e l r f c c c e s e
s a e b t t t m p g
u f t s e i j t u i
l e f e m o c t u o
t c a i m n o h f d
```

Friendship

Friends come in all sizes, shapes, and ages: brothers, sisters, parents, neighbors, good teachers, and school and sports friends.

There is a saying, "To have a friend you need to be a friend." Can you think of a day when someone might have tried to get you to say or do unkind things to someone else? Sometimes it takes courage to be a real friend. Did you have the courage to say no?

A Recipe for Friendship

1 cup of always listening to ideas and stories
2 pounds of never talking behind a friend's back
1 pound of no mean teasing
2 cups of always helping a friend who needs help

Take these ingredients and mix completely together. Add laughter, kindness, hugs, and even tears. Bake for as long as it takes to make your friendship good and strong.

I get by with a little help from my friends.
~ John Lennon

Family Night at the Movies

Rent *Toy Story* or *Toy Story II*. Each movie is a simple, yet powerful, tale about true friendship. Fix a big bowl of popcorn to share with your family during the show.

International Friendship Day

The first Sunday in August is International Friendship Day. This is a perfect day to remember all your friends and how they have helped you during your friendship. Give your friends a call or send them an email or snail-mail card.

Confidence

People are **confident** or have **confidence** when they feel like they can succeed at a certain task. To feel confident about doing something, most people need to practice a task over and over.

Reading, pitching a baseball, writing in cursive, playing the flute, even mopping a floor are all examples of tasks that need to be practiced before people feel confident they can succeed.

What are five things you feel confident doing?

What is one thing you want to feel more confident doing?

Make a plan for how and when you will practice until you feel confident.

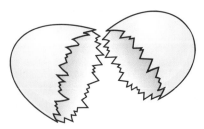

You Crack Me Up!

Materials needed:
1 dozen eggs
a mixing bowl

Cracking eggs without breaking the yolk or getting egg whites all over your hands takes practice.

1. Watch an adult break an egg into the bowl. How did they hold their hands? How did they pull the egg apart?

2. Now you try. Did you do a perfect job the first time? Keep trying until you begin to feel confident about cracking eggs.

3. Use the eggs immediately to make a cheese omelet or custard pie. Refrigerate any unused eggs for up to three days.

Pride

Never bend your head.

Always hold it high.

Look the world

Right in the eye.

~ Helen Keller

Responsibility

You show **responsibility** by doing what you agree or promise to do. It might be a task, such as a homework assignment, or a chore, such as feeding your fish.

When you are young, your parents and teachers will give you simple tasks like putting away toys or brushing your teeth without being asked. As you get older, you will be given more responsibility. You might be trusted to come home from a friend's house at a certain time or drive to the store for groceries.

It takes a lot of practice to grow up to be a responsible person. The easiest way to practice is by keeping your promises and doing what you know is right.

A parent is responsible for different things than a child or a teenager. Write three activities you are responsible for every day. Then write three things a parent is responsible for every day.

If you want your eggs hatched, sit on them yourself. ~ Haitian Proverb

Activity

Materials needed:
21 pennies or counters such as beans, rocks, or marbles
2 small containers labeled #1 and #2

Decide on a reward for successfully completing this activity.
Put all the counters in container #1.
Review the three activities you are responsible for every day.
Each night before you go to bed, put one counter for each completed activity into container #2. At the end of seven days count all the counters in container #2.
If you have 16 or more counters in container #2, you are on your way to becoming very responsible. Collect your reward.

My reward is_____.

Service/Helping

Service is **helping** another person or group of people without asking for any kind of reward or payment. These are some good things that happen when you do service:

1. You feel closer to the people in your community (neighborhood).
2. You feel pride in yourself when you see that you can help other people in need.
3. Your family feels proud of you.
4. You will make new friends as you help others.

An old saying goes, "Charity begins at home." This means that you don't have to do big, important-sounding things to help people. You can start in your own home and neighborhood.

Activity

Each day this week, do one act of service around your house. Don't ask for or take any kind of payment or reward. Be creative! Possible acts of service are

1. Carry in the groceries, do the dishes, or fold the laundry.
2. Read aloud to a younger brother or sister.
3. Make breakfast or pack lunches.
4. Recycle newspapers and cans.
5. Clean the refrigerator or your room.

At the end of the week, think of a project to do with your family that will help your community. You could play musical instruments or sing at a nursing home, set up a lemonade stand and give the money you make to the Special Olympics, offer to play board games with children in the hospital, or pick some flowers and take them to a neighbor. The list goes on and on.

> **All the flowers of tomorrow are in the seeds of today.**
> ~ Indian Proverb

Word Search

Find these words that also mean *service*.

Word Bank		
help	assist	aid
charity	support	boost
benefit	contribute	guide

```
m v l a o d w f d r
c o n t r i b u t e
t b s x c a z v x q
s g p q g w b n y t
i v l y g u v x z i
s n e t e x m n m f
s f h d u d g t e e
a u c h a r i t y n
s u p p o r t u x e
b o o s t g f j g b
```

Honesty and Trust

Being an **honest** person means you don't steal, cheat, or tell lies. **Trust** is when you believe someone will be honest. If you are dishonest, or not truthful, people will not trust you.

You want to tell the truth because it is important to have your family and friends trust you. However, it takes courage to tell the truth, especially if you don't want people to get mad at you or be disappointed in the way you behaved.

How would your parents feel if you lied to them? People almost always find out about lies, and most parents will be more angry about a lie than if you had told them the truth in the first place.

When family or friends ask about something, remember that honesty is telling the truth. Honesty is telling what really happened. Honesty is keeping your promises. *Be proud of being an honest person.*

Write down five feeling words about how you felt when you *weren't* **honest or trusted.**

1
2
3
4
5

Write down five feeling words about how you felt when you *were* **honest or trusted.**

1
2
3
4
5

Parent note: Help your child by pointing out times he or she acted honestly.

Count to Ten

Tape ten pieces of colored paper to your refrigerator. For one week, each time you tell the truth or keep a promise, take one piece of paper down and put it in the recycling bin. If all ten pieces of paper are gone by the end of the week, collect your reward.

Most Improved

Honesty is the first chapter in the book of wisdom.
~Thomas Jefferson

My reward is_____.

Happiness

Happiness is a feeling that comes when you enjoy your life. Different things make different people happy. Some people feel happy when they are playing soccer. Other people feel happy when they are playing the cello. It is important to understand what makes you happy so you can include some of these things in your daily plan.

These are some actions that show you are happy: laughing, giggling, skipping, smiling, and hugging.

Make a list of five activities that make you feel happy.

1.
2.
3.
4.
5.

Bonus!

List two things you could do to make someone else happy.

1._____
2._____

Activity

Write down a plan to do one activity each day this week that makes you happy.

Try simple things—listen to your favorite song, play with a friend, bake muffins, shoot hoops, etc.

Be sure to thank everyone who helps you, and don't forget to laugh!

Happy Thought

The world is so full

of a number of things,

I'm sure we should

all be happy as kings.

~Robert Louis Stevenson

Notes

5 Five things I'm thankful for:

1. _____
2. _____
3. _____
4. _____
5. _____

Notes

5 Five things I'm thankful for:

1. _____
2. _____
3. _____
4. _____
5. _____

Notes

_____

_____

_____

_____

_____

_____

_____

_____

_____

_____

_____

_____

_____

_____

_____

_____

_____

_____

5 Five things I'm thankful for:

1. _____
2. _____
3. _____
4. _____
5. _____

Notes

_____
_____
_____
_____
_____
_____
_____
_____
_____
_____
_____
_____
_____
_____
_____
_____
_____
_____
_____

5 Five things I'm thankful for:

1. _____
2. _____
3. _____
4. _____
5. _____

Congratulations!

_____

your name

HAS COMPLETED

Summer Bridge Activities™

AND IS READY FOR THE 6TH GRADE!

Ms. Hansen

Ms. Hansen

Mr. Fredrickson

Mr. Fredrickson

_____

Parent's Signature

WWW.SUMMER BRIDGE ACTIVITIES.com

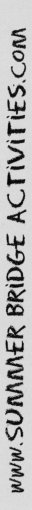